D1391192

The Marvellous Boy

The poet as a legend: 'Chatterton receives the Cup of Poison from the Spirit of Despair', by John Flaxman, circa 1790.

The Marvellous Boy

The Life and Myth of Thomas Chatterton

Linda Kelly

Weidenfeld and Nicolson

5 Winsley Street London W1

ISBN 0 297 00445 X

Printed in Great Britain by The Anchor Press Ltd., and
bound by Wm. Brendon & Son Ltd., both of Tiptree, Essex

For Laurence

I thought of Chatterton, the marvellous Boy,
The sleepless Soul that perished in his pride . . .

Wordsworth, 'Resolution and Independence' (1802)

Contents

Illustrations

The author and publishers are grateful to the following copyright
owners for permission to reproduce the following pictures:
Frontispiece, and facing pages 29 and 44 (*below*), by courtesy of the
Trustees of the British Museum; facing pages 28, 44 (*above*),
45 and 92, by courtesy of the Radio Times Hulton Picture Library;
facing page 93 (*below*), by courtesy of the Bibliothèque Nationale;
facing page 109 (*above*) by courtesy of the Mary Evans Picture Library;
facing page 109 (*below*), by courtesy of the Trustees of the National
Portrait Gallery.

Author's Note

In quoting from Chatterton's Rowley poems I have been faced with the problem of their pseudo-medieval language – under which, in the opinion of Edmund Gosse, his true poetic character is concealed 'as the body of the cuttlefish lies hidden by the profusion of its own ink'. They can be appreciated, in his view, and that of many others, only when the preposterous spelling and wilful archaisms are stripped away. Other critics, Chatterton's biographer Meyerstein among them, hold the opposite view: to tamper with Chatterton's poems, even to alter the spelling, is to deface his genius.

My sympathy is with the purists, but the archaisms can present a barrier to the general reader. In this book I have steered a middle course – quoting the poems in their original form wherever their meaning is clear, using modernized spelling, and occasionally replacing archaisms (usually from Chatterton's own glossary), when they are hard to follow. I quote an example of Chatterton's antique style at its most obscure:

> Al downe in a Delle a merke dernie Delle
> Wheere Coppys eke Thighe Trees ther bee
> There dyd hee perchaunce Isee
> A Damoselle askedde for ayde on her Kne. . .

The modern adaptations of the Rowley Poems are based on those of H. D. Roberts in the 1906 edition of Chatterton's poems. The principal source for the originals has been Tyrwhitt's edition of 1777, but they can be found most conveniently in *The Complete Works of Thomas Chatterton,* edited by Donald S. Taylor in association with Benjamin B. Hoover, published in 1971.

Acknowledgements

I would like to express my thanks to Mr Victor Montagu for allowing me to see family papers relating to Martha Reay; to Miss Joanna Richardson for allowing me to use a quotation from *The Bohemians* (1969) at the opening of Chapter 12; to Monsieur Perrot of the Bibliothèque Nationale for advice on Alfred de Vigny and *Chatterton*; to Mr Nigel Nicolson for allowing me to quote from Vita Sackville-West's *Chatterton*; to Messrs Neville Spearman for allowing me to quote from *Some Poems of E. H. W. Meyerstein* (1960) and *Some Letters of E. H. W. Meyerstein* (1959); and to Professor Lionel Butler for allowing me to quote from his lecture on E. H. W. Meyerstein, delivered at the British Academy in 1955.

Prologue

In 1770 the poet Thomas Chatterton, starving, and defeated in his struggles to succeed as a writer, took poison in his garret room. He was buried in a pauper's grave. Within a few years he had become a legend. Caught up in the dawning Romantic Movement he became a symbol of some of its most powerful preoccupations – suicide, the cult of youth, above all Neglected Genius. He was a stone in the pond; the ripples widened through Romantic art and literature.

He was only seventeen when he died. Of all the Romantic poets who died young he was the first and the youngest. What would he have become if he had lived? He was a prodigy almost without equal in the history of literature. Rimbaud, who abandoned poetry at the age of nineteen, is the nearest parallel. But would Chatterton's precocity have burnt itself out, or might he have developed, as his admirers suggest, to become the greatest of the English Romantic poets? None of his successors – Wordsworth, Coleridge, Shelley, Keats – produced comparable work at the same age.

The question can never be answered. But had Chatterton lived to middle age, however valuable for English poetry, he would never have achieved the mythical renown that he won by his early death.

He was born into the Age of Reason. The Romantic Movement had scarcely begun to stir, the French Revolution, its supposed turning-point, was almost twenty years away when he died. At a time when the influence of Pope was still dominant and the 'virtues of good prose' were those demanded of poetry, his poems, with their imaginative freedom, their bold return to the Gothic past, sounded a prophetic note.

The best of them were forgeries. They were, claimed Chatterton, the work of Thomas Rowley, a fifteenth-century monk, discovered among the documents in the medieval church of Saint Mary Redcliffe, Bristol. It was the age of Ossian and literary impostures. Ignored in Chatterton's lifetime, they became the focus of furious controversy after his death. Were they or were they not medieval? The argument raged for twenty years.

Born out of the publicity surrounding the forgery controversy, the legend of Chatterton himself soon eclipsed it, given an impetus by two important circumstances.

The first was his rejection by Horace Walpole, to whom he had applied, unsuccessfully, for patronage. His subsequent suicide could be laid, though quite unjustly, at Walpole's door. The juxtaposition of scornful aristocrat and starving genius was seized upon by the press. Chatterton's reputation grew as Walpole's was blackened.

Secondly Goethe's *The Sorrows of Werther*, with its justification of romantic suicide, had captured the imagination of Europe and inspired a host of sentimental imitations. Chatterton's suicide (though it took place four years before the book was published) had a fine Wertherian ring, and interpreted thus became a sensational ingredient of Sir Herbert Croft's Wertherian novel *Love and Madness*, a noted bestseller of the 1780s.

By the time the forgery controversy had died down Croft's sentimental view of Chatterton, echoed in poems, prints and paintings, had become the accepted one, and Chatterton's image as a martyred genius was established. His forgeries, hitherto much censured, now became the blueprint for the young Shakespearean forger, William Henry Ireland.

With the turn of the century his myth took on another dimension as the beauty and originality of his poetry began to be appreciated by his poetic legatees. To Wordsworth, Coleridge, Southey, Shelley and above all Keats, who dedicated 'Endymion' to his memory, Chatterton was a source of inspiration not only as a symbol but as a poet.

The death of Keats marked the end of Chatterton's poetic influence, but his legend continued to snowball. 1835 saw the first night of Alfred de Vigny's *Chatterton*, one of the high spots of the French Romantic Theatre, its pale proud hero illustrating the theme of the poet's perpetual victimization by society, a society whose increasing materialism was the fruit of the Industrial Revolution. The play began a craze for suicide *à la Chatterton*. Those were the days, said Theophile Gautier, when poets really did starve in their garrets, and 'you could hear the crack of solitary pistol shots in the night'.

Vigny's plea for Chatterton had been a plea for all poets at odds with the world, his subsequent withdrawal to his ivory tower a symptom, despite his plea, of the growing division between poet and public. His play was the apogee of the Chatterton myth in Europe – but Leoncavallo's opera *Chatterton*, written forty years later and based on Vigny's play, showed its staying power.

In England the morbid aspect of the Chatterton story had a particular attraction for the Pre-Raphaelites, crystallized in Henry Wallis's famous painting 'Chatterton', now in the Tate Gallery. Dante Gabriel Rossetti, in his later years, acquired a passion for Chatterton, identifying with him in his sense of persecution, and dedicating one of his loveliest sonnets to his memory. 'Who is the English poet,' enquired the cynical Count Fosco, villain of Wilkie Collins's *The Woman in White*, 'who has acquired the most sympathy, who makes the finest subject of all for pathetic writing and pathetic painting? . . . That nice young man who started life by forgery and ended it with suicide – your dear, romantic, interesting Chatterton.'

As nineteenth-century Romanticism faded, the image of Chatterton faded too, his last appearance a super-natural intervention as the poet Francis Thompson, drug-ridden and destitute, prepared to commit suicide beneath the arches of Covent Garden. In this century, outside the Romantic Movement, yet linked to it by his feeling for Chatterton, the poet E. H. W. Meyerstein, Chatterton's biographer, has been a lonely champion of his genius.

Today the Chatterton myth has lost its power. The big

questions of the Romantic Movement—what is the poet's role in society? what is society's responsibility to the poet? – are still unsolved, but in England at least they have lost their edge. Poets may face hardship for the sake of their art but it is unlikely that they will starve. The social conditions which defeated Chatterton no longer exist so starkly.

Chatterton's poetry, too, is all but forgotten. There are a few poems in anthologies – one in the *Oxford Book of English Verse*, one in the *Oxford Book of Ballads*; a collected edition of his work has just been published. But, except to specialists, his work is little known. The medieval deception, which agitated eighteenth-century antiquarians and delighted lovers of the Gothic, now works against him. With their archaic language and barbarous spelling the Rowley poems look as hard to read as *Beowulf* – without the justification of antiquity. But if the nettle of their antique style is grasped, their freshness and beauty emerge, foreshadowing the work of the later Romantic poets as primitive Italian painting foreshadows that of the Renaissance. The devotion of Keats and Coleridge, so movingly expressed in their own poetry, is explained; and the core of the Chatterton myth, his poetic genius – without which the Romantic trappings would be irrelevant – is seen to be true.

Part I Life

1 Bristol Childhood

In all his shepen gambols and child's play
In every merry-making, fair or wake
I kenned a purpled light of wisdom's ray
He ate down learning with the wastle cake;
As wise as any of the aldermen,
He'd wit enough to make a mayor at ten.
THOMAS CHATTERTON: 'The Story of William Canynge'

Eighteenth-century Bristol was an unpropitious background for
a poet. It was a pushing, intensely commercial town, counting
itself second only to London in civic dignity, its traditional
prosperity newly augmented by the profits from the slave trade.
Rich merchants, neither cultured nor aristocratic, were the ruling
class. In architecture it was still largely medieval with narrow
streets and stinking gutters. The calm elegance of nearby Bath
seemed far away. Masts of ships crowded the busy harbour; ship
building was a major industry. Shops were clamorous with the
noise of the trades carried on behind their fronts – braziers,
smiths and coopers, tallow candlestick makers and clothiers. 'The
very parsons of Bristol', complained one writer, 'think of nothing
but trade and how to turn the penny.'

Into this hive of business activity Thomas Chatterton was born,
in November 1753. His father, a schoolmaster, had died two
months before, from causes which are unknown. He was a
talented and vital man with interests unusual for his class and time
– antique coins, the occult sciences, the works of the magician
Cornelius Agrippa. He was also an accomplished musician who
sang in the choir of Bristol Cathedral. He had composed an
anthem for his own funeral and in a lighter vein had set his own
verses to a tune for three voices, celebrating a local tavern:

Since now we are met and resolved to be jolly
And drink our Good Liquor to drown Melancholy
Then pass it about, my brave boys, never fear
There's Meat, Drink and Clothes in good Ale and
strong Beer.
While Zealots and Fools with their Factions do
grapple
They taste not the joys which are at the Pineapple.

He was not thought to have been a good husband.

On his death Mrs Chatterton, who was barely twenty, was left almost penniless. With her baby and an elder daughter, Mary, to support, she set up house with her mother-in-law, taking in sewing and running embroidery classes to make ends meet.

Her son was a difficult child, moody, and at first considered so backward that his dame school dismissed him as unteachable. But at the age of six he started to read under his sister's guidance, 'falling in love' with the illuminated capitals in an old music folio of his father's. From then on, scorning modern print, and using a black-letter Bible as his first text book, he became an avid and omnivorous reader, whose curiosity ranged from heraldry and English antiquities to music, metaphysics, mathematics and astronomy. He haunted the Bristol bookshops and circulating libraries.

Through the recommendation of the local vicar a place was found for Chatterton at Colston's Hospital, a charity school for boys destined to become apprentices, and here he was sent as a boarder at the age of eight. The education was confined to English and accounts, a commercial training only being the aim of the founder, along with the inculcation of sound High Tory and Church of England principles. The boys wore the medieval garb of the bluecoat school, with long surcoats and yellow stockings, and their heads were shaven in a tonsure. In this archaic attire, and in the ancient buildings of the school, once a Carmelite priory, lay perhaps the first seeds of Chatterton's identification with a fifteenth-century monk, 'the gode preeste Thomas Rowley'.

Chatterton's eagerness for knowledge was quickly dashed by the limited and unimaginative curriculum. His sister recalled his gloom on arrival at the school; however, she went on to say, 'We remarked he was more cheerful after he began to write poetry.'

At the age of ten, Chatterton's first known poem was published in the local paper, and at just eleven he wrote a 'Hymn for Christmas Day', whose seven stanzas, never faltering into childishness, would not disgrace the *English Hymnal*.

> Almighty framer of the skies
> O let our pure devotion rise
> Like incense in thy sight.
> Wrapt in impenetrable shade
> The texture of our souls were made
> Till thy command gave light . . .

At the same age a satire, 'Apostate Will', provided an early taste of the reverse or scurrilous side of his nature. A turncoat preacher is observed with a beady eye:

> He was a preacher and what not
> As long as money could be got;
> He'd oft profess with holy fire
> 'The labourer's worthy of his hire.'

Chatterton's education, externally uneventful, ended at the age of fourteen when he left Colston's School. On the same day he was indentured to John Lambert, a Bristol attorney, for seven years, the school authorities paying the fees. It was a good place. Most of his fellow pupils had been apprenticed to lowlier trades – grocers, smiths, carpenters and the like. The work of legal copying was light, often taking no more than two hours of the day, and he was free on Sundays and for a few hours every evening. Chatterton, however, chafed under his position, loathing the mechanical work and humiliated at having to eat with the servants and sleep with the pot boy. His master set the footman to keep an eye on him; when he found Chatterton writing poems in the office he would tear them up and fling them in the fire with a cry of 'there is your stuff'.

Lambert himself took little notice of him. He roused himself once to strike him – when he was discovered to be the author of an abusive anonymous letter to his former headmaster – and on another occasion came in on him sitting up late at night, trying to raise spirits from a book of magic. For the rest he remembered him as 'sullen, uncommunicative and visibly contemptuous of others'.

Outside the attorney's office Chatterton cut a more dashing figure. He found friends in a little group of fifteen- and sixteen-year-olds, mostly apprentices like himself. They met to discuss politics and literature, and though inevitably ill-educated and provincial in outlook, they fancied themselves as daring satirists and commentators. Nor were they unsuccessful. Their contributions, though seldom paid for, appeared under imposing pseudonyms in the Bristol papers, and sometimes in the London press as well. The local belles, Miss Rumsey and Miss Hoyland, were the subject of elegant addresses by Chatterton, which also found their way into print:

> Once more the muse to beauteous Hoyland sings;
> Her graceful tribute of harsh numbers brings
> To Hoyland! Nature's richest, sweetest store,
> She made an Hoyland and can make no more ...

Other ladies, less respectable, inspired scraps of obscene doggerel, which shocked Chatterton's Victorian biographers and even now would be considered precocious in a sixteen-year-old. Chatterton's companions were leading him, not unwillingly, into bad ways.

But these temptations and occupations were froth on the surface of his life. They could only be diversions to the boy, already conscious of his genius and obsessed by the dream of the past, which drove him to unremitting work, eating little and sleeping less because, as he said, he did not mean to make himself more stupid than God had intended him to be. The apprentice scribbled in the corner and in the idle hours at Lambert's office the world of Thomas Rowley took shape.

2 Canynge, Rowley and Saint Mary Redcliffe

As onn a hylle one eve sittynge
At oure Ladie's Chyrche mouche wonderynge,
The counynge handieworke so fync
Han well nighe dazeled mine eyne;
Quod I; some counynge fairie hande
Yreer'd this chapelle in this lande;
Full well I wote so fine a syghte
Was ne yreer'd of mortall wighte ...

THOMAS CHATTERTON: 'Onn Oure Ladie's Chyrche'

The church of Saint Mary Redcliffe, Bristol, had been described by Queen Elizabeth I as 'the fairest, goodliest and most famous parish church in England'. Its Gothic minster dominated Redcliffe Hill, where the Chatterton family had its lodgings. For Chatterton, born within the sound of its bells, it was a familiar place from earliest childhood. He would wander for hours in its shadowy interior, studying the medieval tombs and effigies, the intricate stone carvings, the heraldic bearings in the stained-glass windows. As a schoolboy he attended evensong there daily, the vaulted roof dim in the candlelight, choir and organ deepening the sense of Gothic mystery. On summer days he would read in the graveyard, propped up against a tomb; and sometimes he would stretch himself out in the meadows nearby and 'fix his eyes upon the church and seem as if he were in a kind of trance or ecstasy'. It was a passion which would find its deepest expression in his poetry.

For several generations the Chatterton family had been associated with Saint Mary's in the office of sexton, and Mrs Chatterton's brother was the present incumbent. Thanks to this relationship

Chatterton's father had been given permission to remove old records and parchments, considered to be useless, from the muniments room, when the chests containing them had been cleared. He had used them to cover school-books and prize Bibles, and after his death his wife kept the remainder to do duty as spills and thread papers. From such menial uses her son later rescued them, carrying them off to the lumber room which was his only refuge at home, where he would shut himself up mysteriously with inks, charcoal and ochre.

In 1768 the great event of the autumn in Bristol was the opening of the New Bridge. Shortly afterwards, *Felix Farley's Journal*, the principal newspaper of the town, published an account of 'the Mayor's first passing over the Old Bridge, taken from an old manuscript'. The description, with picturesque allusions to 'master Mayor, mounted on a white horse, dight with sable trappings, wroughte by the Nunnes of Saincte Kenna with Gould and Silver' and to 'Preestes and Freeres, all in white Albs, making a most goodlie showe' aroused great interest. The bearer of the transcript, Thomas Chatterton, a sixteen-year-old apprentice, was questioned as to the provenance of the original, and after threats and cajoling admitted that it was one of those taken by his father from the muniments room in Saint Mary Redcliffe. It was in fact his own composition: the first appearance of the so-called Rowley forgeries.

To William Barrett, a local surgeon and antiquarian, who was embarked on an ambitious history of Bristol, the news of this store of hitherto unknown material was hugely exciting. Before long he and two credulous friends, Henry Burgum and George Catcott, were in touch with the youth, who to their delight was able to provide them with transcripts from other, equally notional, originals. Saint Mary's coffers, it appeared, were as inexhaustible as the widow's cruse. Now and then a scrap of ancient parchment, covered with crabbed medieval writing, or a heraldic drawing (the fruit of Chatterton's hours in the lumber room) would provide visible proof of the wonders they had contained.

To Burgum, a pewterer of lowly origins, Chatterton presented his researches into the noble lineage of the De Bergham family, resplendent with a forged coat of arms and the quarterings of distinguished ancestors: 'Azure, three hippopotames naisant Or; Argent, three fermoulxes sable; Or between a fess dancetty sable, two cat a mountains ermine.' This pedigree, dismissed by a disgusted critic as 'a great coat of arms and a string of rubbish, indescribably ignorant and impudent', was swallowed whole by Burgum, who complacently tipped the boy five shillings.

> Gods! What would Burgum give to get a name
> And snatch his blundering dialect from Shame
> What would he give to hand his Memr'y down
> To time's remotest boundary – a Crown.

commented Chatterton sourly.

George Symes Catcott, Burgum's partner, was a well-known Bristol eccentric, who had scaled a church steeple for a bet and preserved all his old teeth in a box labelled, 'My teeth to be put in the coffin when I die'. He wore a cornelian ring in memory of Charles I, a monarch he mourned and revered. Chatterton's medieval discoveries were of just the sort to delight his grasshopper brain, and since Barrett's chief interest was in documents and drawings relating to his history, it was for Catcott that Chatterton first produced his pseudo-antique poetry, in the character of Thomas Rowley, priest, poet and citizen of fifteenth-century Bristol.

Chatterton's Rowley poems, the bane of eighteenth-century scholars and the delight of nineteenth-century Romantics, are his chief claim to fame. They were not written to order. The Rowley cycle had been largely conceived before his gullible patrons came on the scene. One poem at least was composed as early as eleven years old – this, on the evidence of a schoolfellow to whom Chatterton showed his eclogue 'Eleanor and Juga', 'going down Horse Street, near the school, during the summer of 1764'. The fiction of their medieval origins may have started as a sardonic joke against his elders, in which he became too involved to escape, or it may have been a deliberate plan to draw attention to his poetry – poetry which would have been ignored as the work of a mere apprentice. At any rate, spurred on by the interest of the amateur antiquarians, the web of deception became a positive tapestry, and the Rowley poems were released in tantalizing fits and starts against an elaborate background of ancient letters, documents and drawings – with learned footnotes by their editor and discoverer, T. Chatterton.

The scene was Bristol, during the reign of Edward IV, the chronicler Thomas Rowley, and the principal character an actual historical personage, William Canynges Mayor of Bristol, whose effigy lay in Saint Mary Redcliffe, and whose benefactions had helped to build the church. In Chatterton's saga his undoubted virtues were magnified. He was a Maecenas, a merchant prince, patron of art, literature and the Church, whose crowning achievement had been the rebuilding of Saint Mary's,

> The pride of Bristowe and the westerne lande.

Eager for the enlightenment of Bristol he had gathered round him a circle of poets and painters with names culled from tombstones or the realms of fancy: John O'Iscam, Sir Tybalt Gorges, Bishop Carpenter and others. Chief among these phantom characters was the secular monk, Thomas Rowley, a poet whose reputation rivalled that of Chaucer, and Canynge's* confessor and dearest friend.

Rowley's poems and memoirs praised Canynge's munificence, and Saint Mary Redcliffe, its embodiment in stone and symbol of grace:

> But nowe the worde of Godde ys come
> Borne of Mayde Marie toe brynge home
> Mankynde hys shepe
> Them for to kepe
> In the folde of hys heavenlie Kyngedome
>
> Thys Chyrche which Canynge he dyd rear
> To be dispente in Prayse and Prayer
> Mennes souls to save
> From 'vowrynge grave
> And puryfye them Heaven-were.†

---

* Chatterton omits the final 's'.
† 'The Parlyamente of Sprytes'

A lovely poem, 'The Story of William Canynge', using the Early English convention of a 'sweven' or dream, sets out the chronology of Canynge's life. The poet Rowley, grown old and dreaming by the river, sees a vision rising from the water:

> ... a maid
> Whose gentle tresses moved not to the wind
> Like to the silver moon in frosty neet,
> The damoisel did come, so blithe and sweet.
>
> No broided mantle of a scarlet hue
> No shoe peaks plaited o'er with riband gear,
> No costly paraments of woaden blue,
> Nought of a dress but beauty did she wear;
> Naked she was, and lookèd sweet of youth
> All did bewrayen that her name was Truth ...

Truth takes the poet back, the events of Canynge's life are revealed to him in a trance:

> Straight was I carried back to times of yore
> Whilst Canynge swathèd yet in fleshly bed,
> And saw all actions which had been before
> And all the scroll of Fate unravellèd.
> And when the Fate-marked babe a-come to sight,
> I saw him eager gasping after light ...

In the great banqueting hall of Canynge's house the feast days of the Church are celebrated with poems, plays and pageants, written and enacted by Rowley and his fellow poets. Figures from the Scriptures and antiquity mingle quaintly with medieval knights and peasants. Nimrod sings the pleasures of the chase:

> The rampynge lyon, the fell tigère,
> The buck that skips from place to place
> The olyphaunt and rhinocère
> Before me through the greenwood I dyd chase ...*

A ploughman laments his humble lot:

> I rise with the sun
> Like him to drive the wain,

* 'The Parlyamente of Sprytes'

And ere my work is done,
I sing a song or twain.
I follow the plough-tail,
With a long jubb of ale ...

On every saint's high-day
With the minstrel am I seen,
All a-footing it away
With maidens on the green –
But oh! I wish to be more great
In renown, tenure and estate ...*

The background of the Wars of the Roses is sketched in bright impressionistic colours. Maidens lament their lovers slain in battle, shepherds mourn the loss of their pastoral peace:

Oh! I could weep my kingcup-deckèd mees,
My spreading flocks of sheep of lily white,
My tender applynges and embodyde trees,
My parker's grange, far spreading to the sight,
My tender kine, my bullocks strong in fight,
My garden whitened with the comfreie plant,
My flower Saint-Mary shooting with the light,
My store of all the blessings heaven can grant ...†

A fiery ballad, 'The Bristowe Tragedy', describes the execution in Bristol of Sir Charles Bawdin, a Lancastrian knight. (With typical slyness Chatterton's first draft of this had Bawdin's name – recorded in Bristol annals – spelt as 'Bandon'; this seeming misreading from hard-to-decipher manuscript was excitedly corrected by Barrett.)

The feathered songster chaunticleer
Han wound hys bugle horne
And told the earlie villager
The commynge of the morne:

KING EDWARDE saw the ruddie streakes
Of lyghte eclypse the greie

* 'Eclogue the Third'
† 'Eclogue the First'

And herde the raven's crokynge throte
Proclayme the fated daie.

'Thou'rt ryghte' quod hee, 'for, by the Godde
That syttes enthron'd on hyghe!
CHARLES BAWDIN and his fellowes twaine
Todaie shall surelie die'.

'In my humble opinion,' commented Chatterton in a note on the
first verse, 'the foregoing lines are far more elegant and poetical
than all the parade of Auroras clipping the wings of Night,
unbarring the gates of the East, & c. & c.'

A heroic poem in Spenserian stanzas, 'The Battle of Hastings',
is a translation by Rowley from the Saxon of Turgotus, an
eleventh-century monk. ('What I sickened my poor brother with,
I well remember,' recalled Chatterton's sister, 'was my inattention
to "the Battle of Hastings" which before he used to be perpetually
repeating.') It begins with spirit:

O Chryste, it is a grief for me to telle,
How manie a nobil erle and valrous knyghte
In fyghtynge for Kynge Harrold noblie fell,
Al sleyne in Hastyngs feeld in bloudie fyghte.
O sea! our teeming donore han thy floude
Han anie fructuous entendement,
Thou wouldst have rose and sank wyth tydes of
    bloude . . .

Saxon history is the theme, too, of two poetical plays, *Goddwyn*
and *Ælla*, written by Rowley and dedicated to 'the dygne Master
Canynge'. In *Goddwyn*, which is unfinished, the drama centres
round the wise and moderate Goddywn, father of the impetuous
Harold. The scene is the court of Edward the Confessor, where
Norman influence is reaching dangerous proportions. The chorus
in the second act sounds a prophetic note, foreshadowing from
afar the revolutionary fervour of the Romantics:

When Freedom dreste, yn blodde steyned veste
To everie knyghte her warre songe sunge
Uponne her hedde, wylde wedes were spredde,
A gorie anlace bye her honge.

C

She daunced onne the heathe
She hearde the voice of deathe;
Pale-eyned Affryghte hys harte of Sylver hue,
In vayne assayled her bosomme to acale;
She hearde onflemed the shriekynge Voice of Woe,
And Sadnesse ynne the Owlette shake the Dale . . .

Ælla, a completed tragedy, is Chatterton's masterpiece. It describes the struggle of the Saxon hero Ælla against the Danes who threaten Bristol and the West Country, his love for Bertha, his betrayal by Celmonde, his Iago-like lieutenant. The plot is interwoven with songs and lyrics of great beauty, the most famous the 'Minstrels' Roundelay', played to Bertha as she waits in her bower for Aella's return from battle.

O! sing unto my roundelay;
O! drop the briny tear with me;
Dance no more at holy day;
Like a running river be.
My love is dead,
Gone to his death bed,
All under the willow tree.

Black his crine as the winter night,
White his rode as the summer snow,
Red his face as the morning light,
Cold he lies in the grave below;
My love is dead,
Gone to his death bed,
All under the willow tree.

Sweet his tongue as the throstle's note,
Quick in dance as thought can be,
Deft his tabour, cudgel stout,
O! he lies by the willow tree:
My love is dead,
Gone to his death bed,
All under the willow tree.

Hark! the raven flaps his wing,
In the briered dell below;

Hark! the death-owl loud doth sing
To the night-mares as they go;
My love is dead,
Gone to his death bed,
All under the willow tree.

See! the white moon shines on high;
Whiter is my true love's shroud;
Whiter than the morning sky,
Whiter than the evening cloud;
My love is dead,
Gone to his death bed,
All under the willow tree . . .

Come with acorn-cup and thorn,
Drain my hartys blood away;
Life and all its good I scorn,
Dance by night, or feast by day.
My love is dead,
Gone to his death bed,
All under the willow tree.

'Methinks,' wrote Bailey in his recollections of Keats, 'I now hear him recite or *chant* in his peculiar manner, the following stanza of the roundelay, sung by the minstrels in "Ælla": Come with acorn cup and thorn (& c). The first line to his ear possessed the great charm.'

Rowley the poet was Chatterton's second self; the taciturn boy had the secret soul of a medieval monk. In Canynge he created the patron he dreamed of but was never to find, and in the art-loving Bristol of Edward IV an escape from the bustle and commercialism which characterized his native town. His gifts were caught up with the shadow world he had created, and the Rowley cycle was so much his best work that its superiority over his acknowledged poems was the strongest argument of those who after his death refused to believe that he had written them. The point was finally dismissed by Sir Walter Scott: 'He could have had no time for the study of our modern poets . . . while his whole faculties were intensely employed in the Herculean task of creating the person, history and language of an ancient poet, which vast as these faculties were, was sufficient wholly to engross though not to overburden them.'

In forming the pseudo-antique language of Rowley Chatterton's principal sources were Bailey's *Dictionary of Old English*, and Kersey's *Dictionarium Anglo Britannicum*, a highly inaccurate authority in which, said an early critic, he used 'to hunt in the most servile manner'. He also drew on contemporary editions of Chaucer, Spenser and on Percy's *Reliques of Ancient English Poetry* (an important influence), studying their form and metre as carefully as their glossaries. Other sources and reading were of necessity haphazard, dependent mainly on Bristol's circulating libraries, but, in the words of Browning:

Ever in Chatterton did his acquisitions, varied and abundant as they were, do duty so as to seem but a little out of more in reserve. If only a foreign word clung to his memory, he was sure to reproduce it as if a whole language lay behind – setting to work sometimes with the poorest material; like any painter a fathom below ground in the Inquisition, who in his penury of colour turns the weather stains on his dungeon wall into effects of light and shade, and makes the single sputter of red paint in his possession go far indeed.

The story of the Rowley deception was not without precedents. The eighteenth century was rich in successful impostors, whose example could only be encouraging.

Palamazaar, the first and most ridiculous, was a Frenchman who posed as a native of Formosa who had been kidnapped by Jesuits, then escaped to England where he was received into the Protestant Church. He was much fêted, wrote a book about Formosa in Latin, and no one thought the worse of him when his fraud was discovered. He lived to a revered old age: 'I should as soon think of contradicting a bishop,' said Doctor Johnson.

Ossian, the most celebrated impostor of all, was the pseudonym of the Scotsman James Macpherson. The 'Celtic Homer', the third-century bard whose songs he claimed to have discovered in the Highlands, was known all over Europe, translated by Goethe, and later became Napoleon's favourite reading. By the 1760s Macpherson's fortune was made, his pretences slipping as his fame increased.

The year 1765, two years after the publication of Ossian's *Fingal*, saw the appearance of *The Castle of Otranto*, 'translated by William Marshal, Gent, from the original Italian of Onuphrio Muralto', and supposedly first printed 'at Naples in the black letter, in the year, 1529'. The book was a runaway success, and at the second printing the mask was laid aside, and the true author, Horace Walpole, demurely revealed himself.

Macpherson and Walpole were significant figures for other reasons too. The mid-eighteenth century was still the famous 'age of prose and reason'. Pope set the standard of taste in poetry, which, like architecture, was graceful and classical: the Middle Ages were the dark ages, barbarous and odd, Shakespeare only palatable if tidied up and rewritten. Ossian and *Otranto*, with their tales of a non-classical past, were the first cracks in the Palladian façade.

The Ossianic note of wild unspecified yearning, of legend and heroic deeds, marked the earliest reaction against the prosaic temper of the time. The sing-song style, half prophetic, half poetic, was imitated *ad nauseam*, not least by Chatterton:

The noisy thunders roar; the rapid lightnings gleam; the rainy torrents pour and the drooping swain flies over the mountain; swift as Bickerstaff the son of song, when the monster Bumbailiano, keeper of the dark and black cave pursued him over the hills of death and the meadows of dark men! O Ossian! immortal genius! what an invocation could I make now!

Horace Walpole's *Castle of Otranto* was equally a landmark. His romantic medievalism had already found its architectural expression in the charming Gothick of Strawberry Hill. Now it ran riot in a tale of supernatural happenings, a gigantic plumed helmet in the courtyard, a mailed glove in the gallery, a portrait that sighed in its frame, spectral ancestors and mysterious hermits; while the castle itself, with its subterranean vaults and gloomy towers, bore no relation to the smiling porticoes of his contemporaries.

Chatterton had run through Bristol's circulating libraries. He was aware of current fashions, indeed he was a facile imitator, he had gravely marked the success that attended deception. Nonetheless, in Rowley, the eighteenth century was bypassed almost totally. While Ossian's Celtic mists were often unconvincing, and Walpole's Gothick never without its 'k', Chatterton's identification with the Middle Ages was complete and intuitive, seized on since his earliest lessons in the black-letter Bible, and nourished by his near obsession for Saint Mary's. He was a provincial, poor, adolescent, with no cultured circle in which to develop his ideas. His poems gained by his isolation. His sources were Shakespeare, Spenser and Chaucer, and he remained true to them in tone and feeling, turning his back on his own century, and looking forward, though he did not know it, to the Romantic dawn of the next.

'Chatterton can only be underrated,' wrote Rossetti, 'if we expect that he should have done by intuition all that was accomplished by gradual inheritance from *him* half a century later.'

SONGS FROM *Ælla*

Minstrels' Song, by a man and woman

Man   Turn thee to thy shepherd swain,
         Bright sun has not drunk the dew
         From the flowers of yellow hue;
         Turn thee, Alice, back again.

Woman   No, deceiver, I will go,
         Softly tripping o'er the mees,
         Like the silver-footed doe,
         Seeking shelter in green trees ...

Man   Sit thee, Alice, sit and hark,
         How the blackbird chants his note,
         The chelandree, gray morning lark,
         Chanting from their little throat.

Woman   I heard them from each greenwood tree,
         Chanting forth so blatantly,
         Telling lecturnyes to me,
         Mischief is when you are nigh. ...

Man   See the crooking bryony
         Round the poplar twist his spray;
         Round the oak the green ivy
         Flourisheth and liveth aye.

         Let us seat us by this tree,
         Laugh, and sing to loving airs;
         Come, and do not coyen be,
         Nature made all things by pairs.

         Courted cats will after kind;
         Gentle doves will kiss and coo.
Woman   But man, he must be ywrynde
         Till sir priest make one of two.

         Tempt me not to the foul thing,
         I will no man's leman be;
         Till sir priest his song doth sing,
         Thou shalt ne'er find aught of me.

Man   By our Lady her Yborne,
          To-morrow, soon as it is day,
          I'll make thee wife, nor be forsworn,
          So 'tide me life or death for aye . . .

Minstrels' Song

First M.   The budding floweret blushes at the
              light,
           The mees be sprinkled with the yellow
              hue;
           In daisied mantle is the mountain dight,
           The nesh young cowslip bendeth with
              the dew;
           The trees enleafèd, unto heaven
              straught,
           When gentle winds do blow, to
              whistling din is brought.

           The evening comes, and brings the dew
              along;
           The ruddy welkin shineth to the eyne;
           Around the ale-stake minstrels sing the
              song,
           Young ivy round the doorpost do
              entwine;
           I lay me on the grass; yet, to my will,
           Albeit all is fair, there lacketh something
              still.

Second M. So Adam thoughten when, in Paradise,
           All heaven and earth did homage to his
              mind;
           In woman only mannès pleasure lies,
           As instruments of joy were made the
              kind.
           Go, take a wife unto thine arms, and
              see
           Winter, and barren hills, will have a
              charm for thee.

Third M.   When Autumn bleak and sunburnt do
    appear,
With his gold hand gilding the falling
    leaf,
Bringing up Winter to fulfil the year,
Bearing upon his back the ripèd sheaf,
When all the hills with woody seed are
    white,
When lightning-fires and lemes do meet
    from far the sight;

When the fair apple, red as even sky,
Do bend the tree unto the fructyle
    ground,
When juicy pears, and berries of black
    dye,
Do dance in air, and call the eyes
    around;
Then, be the even foul, or even fair,
Methinks my hartys joy is steyncèd
    with some care.

Second M.   Angels be wrought to be of neither
    kind,
Angels alone from hot desire be free,
There is a somewhat ever in the mind,
That, without woman, cannot stillèd be,
No saint in cell, but, having blood and
    tere,
Do find the sprite to joy on sight of
    woman fair.

Women be made, not for themselves,
    but man,
Bone of his bone, and child of his
    desire;
From an ynutyle member first began,
Y-wrought with much of water, little
    fire;
Therefore they seek the fire of love, to
    heat

The milkiness of kind, and make
themselves complete.

Albeit, without women, men were
peers
To savage kind, and would but live to
slay;
But woman oft the sprite of peace so
cheers,
Tochelod in angels' joy they angels be.
Go, take thee quickly to thy bed a
wife,
Be banned, or blessèd hie, in proving
marriage life.

3 The Search for a Patron

Walpole! I thought not I should ever see
So mean a Heart as thine has proved to be;
Thou who in Luxury nursed, beholdst with Scorn
The boy who Friendless, Fatherless, Forlorn,
Asks thy high Favour. Thou mayst call me Cheat –
Say didst thou ne'er indulge in such Deceit?
Who wrote Otranto – but I will not chide
Scorn will repay with Scorn and Pride with Pride ...
Had I the gifts of Wealth and Luxury shared –
Not poor and Mean – Walpole! thou hadst not
    dared
Thus to insult – But I shall live and stand
By Rowley's side when *Thou* art dead and damned.

CHATTERTON's verses on Walpole

Catcott, Barrett and Burgum were willing dupes; they were impressed; they were delighted. But none of this did much for Rowley's creator, who was neither paid for his supposed discoveries, nor helped in finding them a wider public. The antiquarians congratulated themselves on their scholarship, Barrett busily incorporated the results of Chatterton's spurious historical discoveries into his monumental and monumentally boring history of Bristol, and their protégé was considered to be amply rewarded by the interest taken in him by his social superiors, and the privilege of browsing in Barrett's library. It was not enough.

In December 1768 he wrote to James Dodsley, publisher of Percy's *Reliques of Ancient Poetry*, offering to send him copies of ancient poems, 'wrote by one Rowley, a Priest in Bristol'; and six weeks later he sent him an extract from *Ælla* – he would have liked to send the whole of the play, 'but the present possessor absolutely denies to give me one unless I give him a Guinea for a consideration'. This naive request seems to have put off Dodsley; he does not appear to have answered either letter.

Chatterton was not cast down. In the spring of 1769 he decided to present himself to a still higher authority in the antiquarian world – the celebrated Horace Walpole, to whom, as the author of *Otranto*, the idea of a hoax, should it come out, ought not to be repugnant. He accordingly penned the following letter, using Walpole's *Anecdotes of Painting*, the second edition of which had recently appeared, as an opening:

> Sir, Being a little versed in the antiquities I have met with several curious Manuscripts, among which the following may be of service to you, in any feature of your truly entertaining Anecdotes of Painting – In correcting the mistakes (if any) in the Notes you will greatly oblige
> Your most humble servant Thomas Chatterton

Appended to the letter was a sample of Rowley's prose, 'The Ryse of Peycntinge yn Englade' with explanatory notes and a poem by 'Johnne, seconde Abbate of Seyncte Austyns Mynsterre, the fyrste Englyshe paynter yn Oyles' – extracts interesting enough to whet the appetite, but of neither the quality nor the length of that prepared for Dodsley.

To his polite missive Walpole answered by return and with equal courtesy. He confessed himself 'singularly obliged by a gentleman with whom I have not had the pleasure of being acquainted', thanked him for his notes, without which,' since I have not the happiness of understanding the Saxon language', he would not have understood Rowley's text, and expressed interest in further documents: 'Give me leave to ask where Rowley's poems are to be found, I should not be sorry to print them, or at least a specimen of them, if they have never been printed.'

Chatterton's delight can be imagined. Who knows what visions of patronage, of being caught up by this elegant Maecenas, as Rowley was by Canynge, filled his mind? Macpherson had gained fame and fortune through his Ossian impostures; *Otranto* gave him countenance; here perhaps lay his chance to escape from the mediocrity of Bristol and the grudging patronage of Burgum, Barrett and Catcott. He was not slow to reply, sending further samples of Rowley's work. The top of the letter (which Walpole returned and which passed into Barrett's possession after Chatterton's death) has been cut off, but according to Walpole it contained an account of his circumstances and a hint that Walpole might be able to find him a more congenial post. The mutilation is probably Chatterton's – he would have been quick to destroy a paragraph which showed him at a disadvantage. It is certain that he had boasted of his first letter to Barrett, and it is even possible that Barrett may have encouraged him in his application. Walpole's interest in the sources of his history could not fail to add lustre to his work.

But the hopes raised by Walpole's encouraging letter were quickly dashed. Chatterton's second letter, with its ill-advised revelation of his status, alerted Walpole's suspicions. An obliging antiquarian, such as he had assumed, was one thing, an apprentice on the make another. He sent the second samples of Rowley's wares to his friend the poet Thomas Gray. Gray pronounced them modern forgeries and advised Walpole to return them at once.

According to Walpole, he then wrote to Chatterton in kindly terms. He undeceived him as to his being 'a person of any interest' in finding him a post, advised him to continue in his present profession, until he had a sufficient fortune to pursue his antiquarian studies, and reminded him of his filial duty to his mother. 'I also told him that I had communicated his transcripts to better judges and that they were by no means satisfied with the authenticity of his supposed MSS.'

It was not an unreasonable letter. Chatterton's sample of Rowley's work, chiefly in prose, had, unlike that sent to Dodsley, given no sign of his poetic genius; nor had he asked Walpole for money, or claimed to be in need. Walpole had been particularly sensitive to ridicule over antiquarian subjects since he had backed the authenticity of 'Ossian' a few years previously; he may well have suspected that Chatterton was attempting to make him the victim of a hoax.

Chatterton's disappointment was as exaggerated as his hopes. Walpole had used forgery as a literary convention; he had no right, he felt, to condemn him for doing the same. The condescending tone of his letter, the underlying snobbery, convinced him of the true reason for his dismissal: his youth and his humble position. His shame and spleen broke out in verse:

> Walpole, I thought not I should ever see
> So mean a Heart as thine has proved to be ...

He did not send the poem ('My sister persuaded me out of it,' he noted at the foot), but his bitterness revealed itself in his answer to Walpole: 'Though I am but sixteen years of age I have lived long enough to see that poverty attends literature. I am obliged to you sir, for your advice and will go a little beyond it, by destroying all my useless lumber of literature and by never using my pen but in the law.'* It was not a close keeping of Rowley's secret.

Walpole did not reply to the letter, and six days later, having struggled over several drafts, Chatterton wrote more calmly, reiterating his belief in Rowley's antiquity, and requesting the return of his transcripts. This letter, too, Walpole ignored; he was leaving for France, he later explained. After an interval of three months and a further unanswered request, Chatterton wrote again:

Sir, – I cannot reconcile your behaviour to me with the notions I once entertained of you. I think myself injured, Sir; and did not you know my circumstances, you would not dare to treat me thus. I have twice sent for a copy of the MS: – no answer from you. An explanation or excuse for your silence would oblige.

It was a spirited and dignified letter – 'singularly impertinent', in Walpole's view. He sat down to answer, remonstrating with Chatterton – had he not freely offered his transcripts to Walpole? Could he not take further copies from the originals he claimed to have? But on second thoughts, fearing that Chatterton might make use of his letter in print, he flung it aside, half-finished, and snapping up Chatterton's papers in a bundle, despatched them without a covering note.

---

* The letter, additional evidence for those who held the Rowley poems to be forgeries, was not published until 1798, thus after the controversy had subsided.

Chatterton put a good face on his rebuff. It was an amusing literary correspondence 'which ended as most such do', he wrote airily to a friend, though on other occasions he was heard to speak of Walpole 'with a marked degree of acrimony', and in his articles for the London press later on lost no opportunity of lampooning Walpole whenever possible.

But his real revenge would come after his death, when Walpole would be cast in popular opinion as the heartless aristocrat whose neglect had driven him to suicide. 'I am as innocent of the death of Julius Caesar,' Walpole would say indignantly, but the slur remained and has pursued him through posterity.

4 Breaking Away

Since we can die but once, what matters it
If rope or garter, poison, pistol, sword,
Slow wasting sickness, or the sudden burst
Of valve arterial in the noble parts,
Curtail the miseries of human life?
Though varied is the cause, the effect's the same
All to one common dissolution tends.

CHATTERTON: lines from his notebook

Many adolescents at some time or other are drawn to thoughts of suicide. With Chatterton the idea of self-destruction was far more than the usual response to the unhappiness of adolescence. At its root was pride, the pride which was his overwhelming characteristic. He would rather die than fail. Religious scruples faded in comparison. (Chatterton's religious scruples veered widely in any case, from conventional eighteenth-century free-thinking to the belief, expressed in a 'creed' which he habitually carried with him, that 'the Church of Rome (some tricks of priestcraft excepted) is certainly the true Church'.)

Walpole's rebuff had intensified the bitterness and recklessness of his disposition. To the servants at Lambert's he would often talk of his plans to end his life; and several stories, possibly apocryphal, describe his habit of wandering through Bristol with a loaded pistol for this purpose in his pocket.

At the same time he had not given up hopes for the future. Rowley had failed to bring him fame or patronage. He must make his name in the political arena. The stream of medieval poetry ran dry as Chatterton flung himself into political journalism for the London press. For all his ignorance of the world – Bristol worthies ranked as large as Tory ministers – he quickly caught the fashionable tone of cynical invective. His satires on the scandals of his day

Chatterton's Bristol – a view of the harbour with Saint Mary Redcliffe.

The DISTRESSED POET, OR A TRUE

Representation of the unfortunate CHATTERTON

The painting from which the engraving was taken of the distressed poet, was the work of a friend of the unfortunate Chatterton. This friend drew him in the situation in which he is represented in this plate. Anxieties and cares had advanced his life, and given him an older look than was suited to his age. The sorry apartment portrayed in the print, the folded bed, the broken utensil below it, the bottle, the farthing candle, and the disorderly raiment of the bard, are not inventions of fancy. They were realities, and a satire upon an age and a nation of which generosity is doubtless a conspicuous characteristic. But poor Chatterton was born under a sad star; his passions were too impetuous, and in a distracted moment he deprived himself of an existence, which his genius, and the fostering care of the publick, would undoubtedly have rendred comfortable and happy. Unknown and miserable while alive, he now calls forth curiosity and attention. Men of wit and learning employ themselves to celebrate his talents, and to express their approbation of his writings. Hard indeed was his fate, born to adorn the times in which he lived, yet compelled to fall a victim to pride and poverty! His destiny, cruel as it was, gives a charm to his verses, and while the bright thought excites admiration, the recollection of his miseries awakens a tender sympathy and sorrow. Who would not wish that he had been so fortunate, as to relieve a fellow creature so accomplished, from wretchedness, despair, and suicide?

Written on reviewing the PORTRAIT OF CHATTERTON

Ah! what a contrast in that face pourtray'd
Where care and study cast alternate shade
But view it well, and ask thy heart the cause
Then chide, with honest warmth, that cold applause
Which counteracts the soft'ning breath of praise
And shades with cypress the young Poet's bays
Pale and dejected, mark, how genius strives
With poverty, and mark, how well it thrives,
The shabby covering of the gentle bard,
Regard it well, 'tis worthy thy regard,
The friendly cobweb, serving for a screen
The chair, a part of what it once had been,
The bed, whereon th' unhappy victim slept,
And oft unseen, in silent anguish, wept,
Or spent, in dear delusive dreams, the night
To wake, next morning, but to curse the light
Too deep distress the artist's hand reveals
But like a friend, the blackning deed conceals
Thus justice, to mild complacency, bends,
And candour, all harsh inference, suspends
Enthron'd, supreme in judgment, mercy sits
And, in one breath, condemns, applauds, acquits
Whoe'er thou art, that shalt this face survey,
And turn, with cold disgust, thy eyes away,
Then bless thyself, that sloth and ignorance breed
Thee up in safety, and with plenty fed,
Peace to thy mem'ry! may the sable plume
Of dulness, round thy forehead ever bloom
Mayst thou, nor can I wish a greater curse,
Live full disquiet, and die without a nurse.
Or, if some wither'd hag, for sake of hire,
Should wash thy sheets, and cleanse thee from the mire
Let her, when hunger peevishly demands
The dainty morsel from her barb'rous hands
Insult, with hellish mirth, thy craving maw
And snatch it to herself, and call it law
Till pinching famine waste thee to the bone
And break, at last, that solid heart of stone

'Chatterton hankerchiefs', printed in red and blue, were sold at the height of the Rowley Controversy, in 1781.

make indifferent reading now, but of their kind they were polished and vigorous, and before long had brought an encouraging response from the London editors.

Political hack-work provided an admirable outlet for Chatterton's rage against the world, but above all it spelled the chance of escape—escape from the 'damned narrow notions' of Bristol, from the miserable Bristol elders, from the confines of the lawyer's office. Eight months of bombarding the press with contributions saw Chatterton's pieces published in almost all the principal London papers, though the payment, if any, was a bundle of free copies of the paper. Chatterton summed up his connections and decided that the moment had come to try his luck in London itself. Brave plans from a seventeen-year-old apprentice; the struggle for existence in Grub Street, under which the burly figure of Doctor Johnson had all but foundered thirty years before, was still dire. Capricious editors, publishers commissioning work for starvation wages, payments late if at all, were legendary. Hogarth's print 'The Distressed Poet' gave the popular picture.

But for the moment the risks were academic. Chatterton was still an apprentice, unpaid and legally bound by his indentures until 1774. Somehow Lambert must be induced to let him go. In March 1770 Chatterton wrote to a friend threatening suicide in more serious terms than hitherto. The note was intercepted by his master who, greatly alarmed, and knowing Barrett's interest in Chatterton, begged him to remonstrate with him. Chatterton, in tears, seemed to take Barrett's admonitions to heart. He was not in financial distress, he said, he did not drink nor keep bad company.

No; [he wrote to Barrett next day] it is my PRIDE, my damn'd native, unconquerable Pride that plunges me into Distraction. You must know that 19/20ths of my Composition is Pride. I must either live a Slave, a Servant; to have no Will of my own, no Sentiments of my own, which I may freely declare as such; or DIE . . . I will endeavour to learn Humility but it cannot be here.

The last sentence gave the clue. It was Chatterton's menial role in Lambert's office, his lowly status in purse-proud Bristol, that

D

he found intolerable. In London, however poor, he would be free of provincial snobberies.

Lambert's alarm at Chatterton's threat of suicide pointed the way to liberty. A few weeks later, half in bravado, half in earnest, Chatterton wrote another, more elaborate, suicide note, this time left ostentatiously lying on his desk – a Last Will and Testament, giving notice of his intention to kill himself 'on the very next day, Easter Sunday, the Feast of the Resurrection'. Its legacies, written in semi-legal language, were little calculated to win him sympathy:

I give and bequeath all my Vigor and Fire of Youth to Mr George Catcott being sensible he is most in want of it. . . . I give my Abstinence to the Company at the Sheriff's annual feast in General, more particularly to the Aldermen – Item I give and bequeath unto Mr Matt Mease a Mourning ring with this motto Alas! poor Chatterton provided he pays for it himself. Item I leave all the young Ladys the letters they have had from me assuring them that they need be under no Apprehensions from the Appearance of my Ghost for I dye for none of them. . . .

Lambert had had enough. No employer wants the responsibility of a suicide on his premises. Old Mrs Lambert, his mother, had long urged the reality of Chatterton's threats to the servants. Exasperated, he cancelled Chatterton's indentures and dismissed him.

5 The Last Months

Farewell Bristolia's dingy piles of brick
Lovers of Mammon, worshippers of trick!
Ye spurned the boy who gave you ancient lays,
And paid for learning with your empty praise.
Farewell, ye guzzling aldermanic fools,
By Nature fitted for Corruption's tools!
I go to where celestial anthems swell;
But you, when you depart, will sink to Hell.
Farewell, my mother! – cease my anguished soul,
Nor let Distraction's billows o'er me roll! –
Have mercy, Heaven! when here I cease to live,
And this last act of wretchedness forgive.

CHATTERTON's last verses, August 1770

Chatterton was free. Within a few days of Lambert's dismissal he was ready to leave for London. A collection of some five pounds was raised among his friends, Barrett subscribing a guinea. With this small capital and with a bundle of unpublished poems in his bag he bade farewell to Bristol on 17 April 1770; he was never to see it again.

There is no authentic likeness of Chatterton. But we may picture him from contemporary descriptions as he set off: slight, fair-haired, rather slovenly in his dress, with large grey eyes which seemed to flash fire in anger or enthusiasm. His conversation, 'some infidelity excepted, was most captivating'; for all his sullenness he seems to have had great magnetism.

On his arrival in London he quickly made the rounds of the principal London editors: Mr Hamilton of the *Town and Country Magazine*; Mr Edmunds of the *Middlesex*; Mr Fell of the *Freeholders' Magazine*. 'Great encouragement from them; all approved of my design; shall soon be settled,' he wrote to his mother.

He lodged first with a cousin, Mrs Ballance, at the house of Mr Walmsley, a plasterer, in Shoreditch. From the other inhabitants Herbert Croft, enquiring ten years later, was able to obtain first-hand recollections. Mr Walmsley's nephew, with whom Chatterton shared a room, said that 'not withstanding his pride and haughtiness, it was impossible to help liking him – that he lived chiefly upon a bit of bread, or a tart and some water; but he once or twice took a sheep's tongue out of his pocket'. He used to sit up almost all night, reading and writing 'for to be sure he was a spirit and never slept'.

Mr Walmsley's niece said that 'for her part she always took him for a mad boy more than anything else, he would have such flights and vagaries'.

Mrs Ballance described him as:

proud as Lucifer. He very soon quarrelled with her for calling him 'cousin Tommy' and asked if she had ever heard of a poet being called Tommy; but she assured him she knew nothing of poets and only wished he would not set up for a gentleman. Upon her recommending it to him to get into some office he stormed about the room like a madman and said he hoped with the blessing of God, very soon to be sent a prisoner to the Tower which would make his fortune.

Chatterton presumably was thinking of Wilkes, the hero of the hour, whose recent release from prison had been the occasion of public rejoicing. Wilkes, expelled from the House of Commons for criminal libel, and disbarred from Parliament, had been elected while still in prison an Alderman of the City of London – a triumph for the 'patriot' party and a major blow for the King and Tory ministry to whom Wilkes had been a continuing embarrassment since the publication of the notorious No. 45 of the *North Briton,* seven years before.

Chatterton was all for 'Wilkes and Liberty'. Had he not expressed interest in the works of Decimus, Probus and Dunselmus Bristolenus, and amazement at their author's youth? So at least Mr Fell the bookseller had informed him. 'The devil of the matter,' he wrote in swaggering tones to his sister, 'is there's no money to be got of this side of the question. Interest is of the other side. But he is a poor author who cannot write on both sides.'

His hopes of notice, if not of money, however, were pinned on Wilkes's party. At the end of May William Beckford, Lord Mayor of London, a popular figure second only to Wilkes since his support of Wilkes's election to the City, addressed a public remonstrance to the King on Wilkes's continued expulsion from Parliament – forgetting himself so far as to protest extempore when the King, in a prepared reply, remained adamant. This mild breach of etiquette was exalted into an act of heroism by the Opposition press; Chatterton, in the guise of 'Probus', made it the theme of a laudatory epistle addressed to the Mayor, published in the *Middlesex Journal*. In the wake of this timely piece he called on Beckford at the Mansion House, and was flatteringly received by the great man, who promised his backing for a second letter on the subject, this time to appear in the revived, and much more influential, *North Briton*.

It was a marvellous opportunity. Thousands of ambitious Londoners would have given their eyes for such an introduction; Chatterton, a penniless seventeen-year-old, had achieved it within two months of his arrival from Bristol. The publication of his letter, with Beckford's *imprimatur*, could not fail to make his name. But two days before it was due to appear Beckford died suddenly. Chatterton was plunged into despair. According to his cousin's landlady 'when Beckford died he was perfectly frantic and out of his mind and said he was ruined'.

Still reeling from the disappointment he set to work on an elegy on his death instead; and at the end of ten days was able to write on the back of his rejected essay:

Accepted by Bingley, set for and thrown out of the N. Briton, 21 June, on account of the Lord Mayor's death.

	£	s.	d.
Lost by his death on this essay	1	11	6
Gained in Elegies	2	2	0
,, ,, ,,	3	3	0
Am glad he is dead by	3	13	6

But the insouciant note rang somewhat hollow. The payments noted are the only ones recorded for June. Meanwhile the atmosphere had become unpropitious for political writing. Lord North's government, driven too far by Beckford's 'Remonstrance', and by a more than usually scurrilous letter of Junius, were taking steps to coerce the press. The *North Briton* was closed down, the publisher of the *Middlesex Journal* was committed to Newgate, Fell of the *Freeholders' Magazine* was in the King's Bench, other editors, understandably nervous, sheered away from political subjects, and Chatterton found his primary contacts and source of employment gone.

Some time in June, possibly to conceal his growing poverty, perhaps merely in search of privacy, he left the relatively respectable establishment of his cousin and took a room with Mrs Angel, a mantua-maker at 29 Brooke Street in Holborn, then a neighbourhood of dubious character, the haunt of prostitutes and pickpockets. Here, for the first time in his life, he had a room to himself, but here too, ominously, he was out of sight of his relations.

Meanwhile he continued to write with feverish energy. The outlets for political writing being closed, he must set himself to entertain. Under varying *noms de plume* he turned out an extraordinary variety of pieces: witty sketches and short stories, whose characters, with names such as 'Harry Wildfire', 'Flirtilla', 'Tom Goosequill', give an idea of their contents; antiquarian notes; odes and elegies; a lengthy poem, never published, 'The Exhibition', describing the trial of a Bristol clergyman for indecent exposure. 'Would that it had perished,' wrote one biographer, 'with its evidence that youthful purity had been sullied and the precocious boy was only too conversant with forbidden things.'

In a totally different mood, three 'African Eclogues', poems on a semi-mythical Africa – the Tiber is placed on the Gold Coast – had a *Douanier* Rousseau charm. Perhaps Chatterton had watched the slaves on the quays of Bristol and felt their longing for their native land:

> On Tiber's banks where scarlet jasmines bloom
> And purple aloes shed a rich perfume;

> Where, when the sun is melting in his heat,
> The reeking tigers find a cool retreat,
> Bask in the sedges, lose the sultry beam
> And wanton with their shadows in the stream.

By far his most substantial commission and almost the only one for which he received a payment – five guineas – was a pretty burletta, *The Revenge*, written to be performed in Marylebone Gardens. The music has been lost and the piece was never performed, but a song from it, wrote Chatterton to his sister, was a 'great favourite with the town'. The little opera, which Rossetti described as a perfect specimen of Chatterton's acknowledged work, recounts the matrimonial troubles of Juno and Jupiter with interpolations from Cupid and Bacchus. Here, they dispute the rival merits of love and wine:

> *Bacchus*   Since man, as says the bearded sage,
> Is but a piece of clay;
> Whose mystic Moisture's lost by age
> To dust it falls away
> 'Tis Orthodox, beyond a doubt
> That drought will only fret it;
> To make the brittle Stuff last out
> Is thus to drink and wet it . . .
>
> *Cupid*   Hence Monster, hence
> I scorn thy Ivy Crown
> Thy full flowing bowl
> Degenerates the soul;
> It puts our judgement down
> And prostitutes the sense.
>
> *Bacchus*   Gadso, methinks the youngster's woundy
>   moral –
> He plays with Ethics like a Bell and Coral.

Of Rowley during this London period there was only one appearance. Rowley was a creature conceived during the leisurely hours in Lambert's office. He could have little place among the hectic rush and scramble of Chatterton's London life when writing was his only means of support and the proportion of pot-boilers was high. But he makes his final appearance, a few weeks before

Chatterton's death, in the grave and lovely 'Ballade of Charitie', his swan song and Chatterton's own.

The payment for *The Revenge*, received on 6 July, was Chatterton's last windfall. He spent much of it straight away on a box of presents for his family: a set of china, a snuff box and two fans for his mother and grandmother; for his sister there was a promise of silks:

You have your choice of two. I am surprised that you chose purple and gold; I went into the shop to buy it; but it is the most disagreeable colour I ever saw; dead, lifeless and inelegant. Purple and pink, or lemon and pink are more genteel and lively. Your answer in this affair will oblige.

The presents were a gesture of bravado. Four months of literary drudgery had brought little reward. Editors, besieged by would-be journalists, were in no hurry to pay their contributors. Chatterton, as he grew shabbier and more insistent, found himself dismissed as importunate. In a fit of desperation he had written to Barrett, begging him to use his interest to find him a place as a ship's surgeon – he had picked up some rudiments of medicine in Barrett's library – but Barrett ignored his request and the cry for help which underlay it.

August was a dead month in London. The taverns and coffee-houses, with their chances of contacts, were emptying, no more commissions were forthcoming. As the month wore on Chatterton was at last in actual need; the brave hopes and the brave boasts with which he had left Bristol proved without foundation. The pride which had sustained him so far was now a stumbling block; he could yet have survived had he taken some menial appointment, but he would not humble himself to do so.

Most evenings of his last few weeks he would step into the shop of Mr Cross, the local chemist, to chat, his old charm still evident, as he talked in sweeping terms of religion, philosophy, politics. Mr Cross, seeing his straits, would try to press him to a meal, but he persistently refused all invitations, frailty overcoming him only once when he consented to share a barrel of oysters, which he was observed to eat 'most voraciously'.

The day before he died his landlady, knowing that he had not eaten for two or three days, begged him to take some dinner with her, but he was offended at her expressions, which seemed to hint that he was in want, and assured her that he was not hungry. The dashing of his hopes, the pangs of hunger and penury may well have been enough for one to whom suicide was no new idea, but it seems likely too that he was suffering from venereal disease, of which the current cure, using vitriol, could be agonisingly painful. 'Mr Cross says he had the foul disease which he would cure himself and had calomel and vitriol of Cross for that purpose who cautioned him against the too free use of the same.'*

On the morning of 24 August he was found dead in his room having taken arsenic and water, a distorted and ghastly figure, lying in his own vomit – a far cry from the beautiful youth of the famous pre-Raphaelite painting. Scattered across the room were scraps of paper torn into tiny pieces, a last poem perhaps, torn up in frustration and despair. He was seventeen and nine months old.

* Memorandum of Michael Lort, the eighteenth-century antiquarian, in Bristol Central Library.

An Excellent Ballad of Charity
As wroten bie The Gode Preeste Thomas Rowley, 1464

In Virginè the sultry sun 'gan sheene,
And hot upon the meads did cast his ray:
The apple ruddied from its paly green,
And the soft pear did bend the leafy spray;
The pied chèlandry sang the livelong day:
'Twas now the pride, the manhood of the year,
And eke the ground was dight in its most deft
   aumere.

The sun was gleaming in the mid of day,
Dead still the air and eke the welkin blue,
When from the sea arist in drear array
A heap of clouds of sable sullen hue,
The which full fast unto the woodland drew,
Hiding at once the Sunnè's festive face;
And the black tempest swelled and gathered up
   apace.

Beneath an holm, fast by a pathway side,
Which did unto Saint Goddwyn's convent lead,
A hapless pilgrim moaning did abide,
Poor in his view, ungentle in his weed,
Long breastful of the miseries of need.
Where from the hailstorm could the beggar fly?
He had no housen there, nor any convent nigh.

Look in his gloomèd face; his spirite there scan,
How woebegone, how withered, sapless, dead!
Haste to the church glebe-house, accursed man,
Haste to thy coffin, thy sole slumbering bed!
Cold as the clay which will grow on thy head,
Are Charity and Love among high elves;
Knightis and Barons live for pleasure and themselves.

The gathered storm is ripe; the big drops fall;
The sunburnt meadows smoke and drink the rain;
The coming ghastness doth the cattle 'pall,
And the full flocks are driving o'er the plain;

Dashed from the clouds the waters gush again;
The welkin opes, the yellow lightning flies;
And the hot fiery steam in the wide flame-lowe dies.

List! now the thunder's rattling clamouring sound
Moves slowly on, and then upswollen clangs,
Shakes the high spire, and lost, dispended, drown'd
Still on the frighted ear of terror hangs;
The winds are up; the lofty elm tree swangs;
Again the lightning and the thunder pours,
And the full clouds are burst at once in stormy
    showers.

Spurring his palfrey o'er the watery plain,
The Abbott of Saint Goddwyn's convent came;
His chapornette was drenched with the rain,
His painted girdle met with mickle shame;
He backwards told his bederoll at the same;
The storm increasèd, and he drew aside,
With the poor alms-craver near the holm to bide.

His cope was all of Lincoln cloth so fine
With a gold button fastened near his chin;
His autremete was edged with golden twine,
And his shoe peaks a loverde's might have been.
Full well it showed he thoughten cost no sin:
The trammels of the palfrey pleased his sight,
For the horse-milliner his head with roses dight.

'An alms, Sir Priest!' the drooping pilgrim said,
'O! let me wait within your convent-door
Till the sun shineth high above our head
And the loud tempest of the air is o'er;
Helpless and old am I, alas! and poor;
No house, nor friend, nor money in my pouch;
All that I call my own is this my silver crouch.'

'Varlet,' replied the Abbot, 'cease your din;
This is no season alms and prayers to give;
My porter never lets a beggar in;
None touch my ring who not in honour live.'

And now the sun with the black clouds did strive,
And shot upon the ground his glaring ray;
The Abbot spurred his steed, and eftsoons rode
  away.

Once more the sky was black, the thunder roll'd:
Fast running o'er the plain a priest was seen,
Not dight full proud nor buttoned up in gold;
His cope and jape were grey, and eke were clean;
A Limitour he was, of order seen;
And from the pathway side then turned he,
Where the poor beggar lay beneath the holmen
  tree.

'An alms, Sir Priest,' the drooping pilgrim said,
'For sweet Saint Mary and your order's sake!'
The Limitour then loosened his pouch thread
And did thereout a groat of silver take;
The needy pilgrim did for gladness shake.
'Here, take this silver, it may ease thy care;
We are God's stewards all, – nought of our own
  we bear.

But ah! unhappy pilgrim, learn of me,
Scarce any give a rent roll to their Lord:
Here take my semicope, – thou'rt bare, I see;
'Tis thine; the Saints will give me my reward!
Virgin and holy Saint who sit in gloure,
He left the pilgrim and his way aborde.
Or give the mighty will, or give the good man
  power!'

Part II   Controversy

6 The Rowley Controversy

Gentlemen of the jury, the prisoner at the bar, Thomas Chatterton, is indicted for the uttering of certain poems composed by himself, purporting them to be the poems of one Thomas Rowley, a priest of the XVth century, against the so frequently disturbed peace of Parnassus, to the great disturbance and confusion of the antiquary society and likewise notoriously to the prejudice of the literary fame of the said Thomas Chatterton. The fact is stated to have been committed by the prisoner between the ages of fifteen and seventeen and the poems are admitted to be excellent.

'Trial of Thomas Chatterton', *The New Review* (1782)

The death of Chatterton caused little stir. The inquest was purely formal, the verdict was 'suicide by reason of insanity', and the body, having been enclosed in a parish shell, was buried in the graveyard adjoining Shoe Lane workhouse. The newspapers he had courted so assiduously were dumb, though they continued to use, gratis, such contributions from his pen as they had in hand. It was not until October, two months after his death, that a solitary voice was raised in public mourning when the *Town and Country Magazine* published an elegy, twenty-three verses long, by Thomas Cary, a literary youth and a friend of Chatterton's Bristol days:

> Weep, nature, weep, the mighty loss bewail,
> The wonder of our drooping isle is dead;
> Oh could but tears or plaintive sighs avail,
> By night and day I would bedew my bed ...

But meanwhile, only a few days too late, a patron such as Chatterton had vainly sought in life had appeared in Bristol. He was Doctor Thomas Fry, a former pupil of Bristol Grammar

School and now head of Saint John's College, Oxford. He had returned to his native town with the express intention of finding out more about the ancient poetry discovered there, of which rumours had reached Oxford, and thereafter of patronizing Chatterton, whether as their author or discoverer only, should he be in need. He was informed that Chatterton had gone to London, where he had recently destroyed himself.

The news did not abate his curiosity. He called on Barrett and Catcott and took away transcripts of the poems in Chatterton's handwriting, promising to return them when he had studied them and made a glossary. Thus began a thriving trade in Chatterton manuscripts which snowballed as interest in the Rowley poems grew, fanned by the controversy which soon arose as to their authorship. Catcott, as owner of most of Chatterton's poetic 'transcripts' (with Barrett concentrating on documents relating to his history of Bristol), was the chief beneficiary. Shortly afterwards he shrewdly added to his store by buying from Mrs Chatterton, for £5, such copies of her son's poems as remained in her possession.

Interest in the poems, circulating among Doctor Fry's academic friends, grew quickly and before long they had become a talking-point in literary circles not only in Oxford but in London. Their beauty and originality were immediately recognized as critics more fitted to appreciate them than Barrett and Catcott read and discussed them with amazement. But were they genuinely medieval, as the Bristol elders maintained? There was no reference to Rowley in any document of his supposed period; there were curiously familiar echoes from later authors, Spenser, Shakespeare and even Pope, in some of the poems. On the other hand it seemed scarcely possible that Chatterton, a teenage apprentice with a minimal education, could be the composer of works so full of genius and erudition.

Doctor Johnson, though he had early decided that the poems were modern, summed up the critics' dilemma:

It is a sword that cuts both ways. It is as wonderful to suppose that a boy of sixteen had stored his mind with such a train of images and ideas as he had acquired, as to suppose the poems with their ease of

Being versed a little in antiquity, I have met with several curious Manuscripts among which the following may be of service to you in any future Edition of your truly — taining Anecdotes of Painting — In correcting the Mistakes (if any) in the Notose you greatly oblige

Your most humble Servant.

Thomas Chatterton
Bristol March 25
Corn Street

The Ryse of Peyncteynge, yn Englade, wroten bie T. Rowleie. 1469 for Mastre Canynge.

Rowleie was a Secular Priest of St. John's, in this City. his Merit as a Biographer istoriographer is great, as a Poet still greater: some of his Pieces would do honor ne; and the Person under whose Patronage they may appear to the World, will lay Englishman, the Antiquary, and the Poet, under an eternal Obligation —

Chatterton's first application to Horace Walpole, 25 March 1769.

'The Death of Chatterton', by Edward Orme, engraved in 1794.

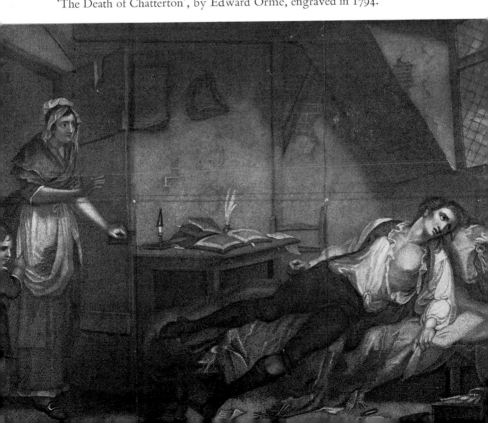

The Chatterton Monument – 'a rude but substantial Gothic arch raised between the bosom of two hills'. From the *Ladies Magazine*, 1784.

versification and elegance of language, to have been written by Rowlie in the time of Edward the Fourth.

Catcott and Barrett became the centre of attention as learned enquirers, wishing to know more of the Rowley poems, descended on Bristol, Barrett secretive and grudging with his time, Catcott glorying in his role as 'Rowley's midwife'. 'You must know,' wrote one visitor, 'that this Catcott is a pewterer, and though very fond of scribbling, especially since he got Rowley's works, is extremely ignorant and illiterate. He is however very vain and fancies himself as great a genius as Rowley himself.'

For all his enthusiasm there was a certain ambivalence in Catcott's attitude to his poems. He liked to surround them with an air of mystery, seldom allowing more than one to be seen at a time and extracting promises of discretion from those who took copies. He was reluctant to allow them to be published, until his friend Doctor Barrett's *History of Bristol* appeared – the reluctance to anticipate him strengthened, possibly, by some question of joint ownership.

Nowhere was his ambivalence – and Barrett's – more marked then in his attitude to the parchment 'originals' (as opposed to 'transcripts' in Chatterton's own writing) of the Rowley manuscripts. Expert examination of these would have done more than any other factor to establish the authenticity or otherwise of the poems. Nonetheless they were unwilling to submit them to it. Barrett indeed, to Catcott's displeasure, was persuaded by Lord Dacre, one of several 'noble lords' who had flattered the pair with their visits, to lend him two fragments of parchment to be sent to Thomas Percy – editor of the *Reliques of Ancient Poetry* and an authority on old manuscripts – for an opinion. Percy had no hesitation in pronouncing them modern forgeries. Unfortunately, to the confusion of Percy and Lord Dacre, the parchments were mislaid before they could be returned. This circumstance, said Catcott darkly, did much to invalidate Percy's conclusions. Barrett, displeased by the opinion still more than the loss, resolved to lend no more.

Meanwhile the authorities at Saint Mary Redcliffe, alarmed at the thought that valuable documents had slipped through their hands, closed the chests in the church with lock and key, and sent a stern request to Mrs Chatterton to return any manuscripts remaining in her possession.

Doctor Johnson went down to Bristol with Boswell to investigate. His encounter with Catcott confirmed his scepticism. The worthy pewterer called on them at their inn (an inn so bad, said Doctor Johnson jokingly, 'that Boswell wished to be in Scotland'). 'I'll make Doctor Johnson a convert,' he called out with a triumphant air. While Johnson at his desire read aloud some of the Rowley verses Catcott stood at the back of his chair, 'moving himself like a pendulum and beating time with his feet and now and then looking into Doctor Johnson's face and wondering he was not convinced'. Later, after a visit to Barrett, who allowed a fleeting glimpse of his 'originals', Catcott insisted that they should see with their own eyes the ancient chest in which the Rowley poems were found. Doctor Johnson good-naturedly agreed, and laboured up the stairs to the muniments room, puffing and blowing. 'There,' said Catcott with a bouncing, confident credulity, '*there* is the very chest itself.' After this ocular demonstration, wrote Boswell, there was nothing more to be said.

'This is the most extraordinary young man that has come to my knowledge,' remarked Doctor Johnson afterwards, 'it is wonderful how the whelp has written such things.' Nonetheless he had little sympathy for Chatterton. 'Pho, don't talk to me of that vulgar uneducated stripling,' he snorted on another occasion when the boy poet's praises were sung. Nor did he include him when he edited his *Lives of the Poets*, though space was found for many a lesser figure, now deservedly forgotten. Did he bear a grudge against Chatterton, who in his poem 'Kew Gardens' had attacked him in terms of staggering vulgarity, as a Tory Party hack who had betrayed his genius for a government pension? A typical couplet,

> Whilst from his fancy figures budded out
> As hairs from humid carcases will sprout

gives the flavour. An embarrassing evening at Mrs Thrale's is described in Fanny Burney's diary, when Michael Lort, the antiquarian, gave a reading from some of Chatterton's modern poetry. When he reached the passages on Doctor Johnson he continued reading, 'with a steady voice and unmoved countenance'. Mrs Thrale looked displeased, the other guests were abashed or secretly smiling. Doctor Johnson listened with an air of profound attention, and laughed heartily. The laughter was perhaps a little forced.

In 1776, shortly after Johnson's visit to Bristol, Thomas Tyrwhitt, the eminent scholar and editor of Chaucer, set off to make his own enquiries. He had recently come to an arrangement with Catcott, through intermediaries, to edit and publish the first collected edition of the Rowley poems, which (apart from the *Bristowe Tragedie* published privately by Catcott) had never before appeared in print. Catcott's scruples about allowing the poems to be published before the appearance of Barrett's history had been overcome: partly by Barrett's procrastination – his history showed no sign of ever being finished; partly by a handsome payment; and, most importantly, with so many copies circulating in manuscript, by fear of a pirate edition appearing should he delay much longer.

Tyrwhitt at this time believed the Rowley poems to be genuine – he had even used quotations from them in his notes on Chaucer. He checked on Johnson's views before he left, and was shaken by his scoffing dismissal of Rowley's claims. His six days in Bristol, discussing and examining the poems with Catcott and Barrett, did still more to undermine his faith. By the time the collected edition appeared, in 1777, his original position was reversed. Careful study of the poems, on the basis of style and vocabulary, had convinced him that they were modern forgeries.

However, despite his private conviction, both the first and second edition of the poems were published with a non-committal introduction in which he left the determination of their authorship to 'the unprejudiced and intelligent reader'. The question must be determined, he said, first by the examination of the fragments of vellum in Barrett's possession, though their authenticity did not presuppose that of the other poems, of which only transcripts existed, and secondly on the internal evidence.

The debate was now thrown open, and the controversy, hitherto confined to academic circles, became a matter of general interest, with newspapers and magazines standing on the sidelines as warring scholars – those who believed the Rowley poems ancient and those who thought them modern – warmed for the battle. Though the finest antiquarians of the day, Percy, Edward Malone, the Shakespearean scholar, and Thomas Warton, the medievalist, were convinced on the basis of style alone that the poems were forgeries, they were confronted by a powerful and vociferous opposition who took their authenticity as a point of honour. Despite the learned paraphernalia which they brought to bear on the question, their biggest stumbling-block was one of social and intellectual snobbery. That Chatterton, ill-bred and ill-educated, should be the possessor of genius ran contrary to all their prejudices. It was no coincidence that the two most ardent supporters of Rowley, Jacob Bryant and Dean Milles, President of the Society of Antiquaries, were possessed of impeccable social and academic connections. Catcott, who had been much put out by the way his 'ingenious arguments' had been ignored in Tyrwhitt's preface, joined them in pointing out 'the glaring absurdity of supposing that a boy of fifteen, bred up in a charity school, totally deprived of the advantages of Classical Learning', could have composed the poems.

The following year, 1778, the publication of *Chatterton's Miscellanies*, a collection of his modern verse and prose, took some of the steam out of their arguments by demonstrating that Chatterton's acknowledged work was at least comparable to the Rowley poems. In the same year, Tyrwhitt, in the third edition of the Rowley poems, included an appendix in which he stated his conviction that the poems were entirely modern; and Thomas Warton, repeating the same conclusion in his *History of Modern Poetry* shortly after, satirized those who sneered at Chatterton's birth and education: 'How could that idle and illiterate fellow Shakespeare, who was driven out of Warwickshire for stealing, write the tragedy of Othello?'

At this Jacob Bryant rumbled into the attack, assisted by his friend Doctor Glynn of King's College, Cambridge, who 'affirmed that he could as soon believe the moon was made of green cheese' as admit that the poems were the work of Chatterton. His two-volume dissertation proving the poems' antiquity, backed with innumerable examples from Anglo-Saxon literature, has been rightly described as 'a monument of perverted ingenuity'. 'I cannot wade through.all that mass of old English and authors,' wrote Horace Walpole. 'Any man can convince me if he write but long enough and dully enough for I had rather believe than read.'

Bryant's ponderous work was followed in 1782 by another still more weighty defence of Rowley: Dean Milles's rival edition of Rowley's poems, clearly intended to be definitive, the text almost buried under the weight of the commentary.

Both Malone and Tyrwhitt riposted before the year was out, and the battle which ensued outshadowed all other literary topics. Pamphlets flew between the opposing parties, the Chattertonians excelling themselves in satire, those of the Rowley persuasion, too deeply involved to have a sense of humour, responding with ever murkier appeals to ancient precedents.

The principal arguments of the Rowley side were these: first, that the parchments produced by Chatterton were undoubtedly antique, and there had been documents of the Rowley period in Saint Mary's; secondly, the poems contained little-known historical facts and rare and obsolete words which Chatterton with his limited sources of information could not have known; thirdly, that it was impossible that he should have had the time, either at school or in the attorney's office, to compose such a body of work. Moreover, they argued, it was psychologically impossible that Chatterton, with his burning ambition and desire for fame, should not have claimed their authorship had they been his work.

To these the anti-Rowleians replied; first, that the Rowley poems were 'transcripts' and only a few parchment 'originals' existed – at the bottom of each sheet of ancient deeds discovered in the chest in Saint Mary's there was usually a blank space of four or five inches in depth and this exactly agreed with the size of the largest fragments of parchment which Barrett had allowed to be seen; secondly, the knowledge of archaic words and rare facts, though amazing, could have been obtained from sources available in Bristol. There was an equal number of historical inaccuracies in the poems too, as for example a reference to knitting in *Ælla*:

> As Elynour bie the green lesselle was syttynge,
> As from the sone's hete she harried,
> She sayde as her whytte hands whytte hosen was
>   knyttynge,
> What pleasure ytt ys to be married,

when it was an established fact that the art of knitting was unknown in the reign of Edward IV. The third point, that of time, was a matter of opinion; Chatterton's immense output of work in his four months in London evidenced an extraordinary facility and speed. The psychological question was one of opinion too: Chatterton's character could be interpreted in many ways.

Even in an age when critical scholarship was in its infancy the arguments of the anti-Rowleians carried conviction, and though the controversy simmered on for many years – the last pamphlet attempting to prove the poems medieval appeared in 1857 – Dean Milles and his supporters were generally considered to have been routed by the end of the 1780s. Long before that the public had grown heartily sick of the subject. An irritated correspondent to Mr Urban, editor of the *Gentleman's Magazine*, summed up the general feeling:

> Still Chatterton, Rowley, Milles and old Bryant,
> Will you never be done, Mr Urban? O fie on't.
> All methods of cooking to dress them you've tried
> You have stewed, fricaseed and have broiled them
>   besides
> It is time to give over for what can avail
> The best season'd sauce when the meat is quite
>   stale.

The forgery question had indeed grown stale, but Chatterton himself was moving from the realms of controversy to those of myth. Ironically, it was Horace Walpole who, by his supposed neglect of genius, gave the preliminary impetus to his legend.

7 The Embarrassed Dilettante

Unfortunate boy! Short and evil were thy days, but thy fame shall be immortal. Hadst thou been known to the munificent patrons of genius – But wast thou not known to one? If fame report thy conduct truly it was not kind of thee, Horatio. . . . Wast thou not considered as the oracle of taste, the investigator of all that is curious in art and literature. . . . It was then at last thy only pride and pleasure to bring to light a catalogue of royal and noble authors. What hast thou to do with reptile, with a poor friendless and obscure charity boy? Besides, exclaims Horatio, it was a forgery . . . a horrid vile forgery. . . . Impostors are not to be encouraged. But let us ask thee, didst thou not put a false name to thy own romance. . . . If indeed thy neglect of the poor boy arose from mistake and inadvertancy and I think it might, the generous Publick freely forgive thee . . . but if from Pride and Insolence, the present and all future times will properly resent an omission, which hastened one of the greatest geniuses England ever knew to that bourne from which no traveller returns.

REV. VICESIMUS KNOX: *Essays Moral and Literary* (1782)

In April 1771, eight months after Chatterton's death, Horace Walpole had been a guest at the inaugural banquet of the Royal Academy, an important event attended by most of the leading figures in the arts. Sir Joshua Reynolds presided, and Doctor Johnson and Oliver Goldsmith were among the company. Theirs was not a set in which Walpole, snobbish about other authors, habitually moved: 'I shun authors and would never have become one myself had it obliged me to keep such bad company.' But at dinner, being placed near them, he was intrigued to hear Oliver Goldsmith, who was planning to visit Bristol to see it, in great excitement over a treasure of ancient poetry there, while Doctor Johnson laughed at his credulity.

Walpole, realizing that this was 'the *trouvaille* of my friend

Chatterton', archly announced that the news was no news to him, who might, had he wished, 'have had the honour of announcing the great discovery to the learned world'. But his mirth was soon dashed when on enquiring about Chatterton he was informed that he had committed suicide. Chatterton, added Goldsmith, was known as the 'young villain' in Bristol, and at the time of his death had been far gone in the 'venereal disorder'.

Goldsmith's visit to Bristol later was not a success. He called on Catcott, with an offer of £200 for his manuscripts; Catcott had better plans for his treasure. 'Alas Sir,' he replied, 'I fear a poet's note of hand is not very current upon our exchange of Bristol.'

As the Rowley controversy developed Horace Walpole, though never in doubt as to the authorship of the poems, became increasingly involved, first as spectator, then, unwillingly, as actor. He was profoundly struck by the beauty of Rowley's verse – which none of the pieces Chatterton sent to him could have led him to expect – and, far more than the churlish Doctor Johnson, gave Chatterton his posthumous due. 'For Chatterton, he was a colossal genius and might have soared I know not whither,' he wrote to the Countess of Upper Ossory; and at his death a collection of eighteen volumes of material on Chatterton, poems and cuttings relating to the controversy, was among the lots in the sale of his books and papers. But from the Academy dinner onwards he had been uneasy as to what might be said of his own relations with Chatterton. His conscience was clear, he insisted, but he had, with reason as it turned out, a deep distrust of what the press might make of them.

When Tyrwhitt's edition of the poems appeared in 1777 he was relieved to see no mention of his name in the introduction. But his relief was short-lived. A review of the book, appearing in the *Monthly Review*, noted the fact that Chatterton had been given no encouragement by Walpole, as a strong argument against the poem's authenticity. There was nothing startling about this, but in the following month, Catcott, in an article in the same magazine, again linked Walpole's name with Chatterton, this time in a calamitous way. Chatterton, wrote Catcott, had taken his manuscripts to London in the hope of disposing of them there. 'He accordingly applied, as I have been informed, to that learned antiquary, Mr Horace Walpole, but met with little or no encouragement from him, soon after which, in a fit of despair, as it is supposed, he put an end to his unhappy life. . . .'

This was the purest calumny. Chatterton had applied to Walpole eighteen months before his death, when he was still in Bristol, and by his own account in no need of money. But Catcott's account, as Walpole's friend George Cole wrote to him solicitiously, might be 'construed into homicide' against him. It was. The juxtaposition of Chatterton, the struggling young apprentice, with Walpole, rich, famous and aristocratic, added new spice to the Rowley debate. The imputation that Walpole, popularly cast as a heartless dilettante, had occasioned Chatterton's death by his neglect, was picked up and repeated by journalists, whose love of sensation was joined with envy of Walpole's position. Chatterton's character, which till then had had few defenders, was progressively whitened as Walpole's actions were made more black. Goldsmith's 'young villain' was becoming a martyr.

Walpole, who at first felt it more dignified to refrain from answering his accusers, was at last constrained to defend himself in print. He set out the full story of his transactions with Chatterton in a privately printed pamphlet. Two hundred copies were circulated, but, as these proved inadequate to stem the rising tide of criticism, he was driven to make the pamphlet public, and, in 1782, his account of his correspondence with Chatterton was published in four consecutive issues of the *Gentleman's Magazine*. He described his reception of Chatterton's letter, his subsequent conviction that the samples were spurious, his distress in learning of his fate, his present admiration of his genius. He had never believed in the fifteenth-century Rowley, but was lost in wonder at the thoroughness of Chatterton's deception, 'who before twenty-two could create a language that all the learned of Europe, though they suspected, could not detect'. But all the effect of praise and truthful explanation was undone in one blow, when Walpole, grown peevish from a sense of injured innocence, remarked of Chatterton's forgeries: 'All of the house of forgery are relations . . . his ingenuity in counterfeiting styles, and I believe, hands, might easily have led him to those more facile imitations of prose, promissory notes' – an accusation as unfounded as the one that he himself had caused Chatterton's death, and especially inappropriate from the author of *Otranto*.

Walpole's answer to his critics did not silence them. The ill-judged remark about forgery was not allowed to be forgotten. An anonymous pamphlet, published the same year, congratulated him on having acted 'considerately and *humanely*' in suffering Chatterton to starve, seeing that he might otherwise have taken to crime: and Dr Vicesimus Knox's fervent reproaches followed shortly after. As the sniping attacks continued Walpole began to realize that, whatever his protestations of innocence, his name was indissolubly linked with Chatterton's.

Of course he had his defenders too. The whitewashing of Chatterton's character was not yet complete. 'A youth is dead,' wrote Walpole's friend Mason,

> . . . felo da se or not
> By pox or poison matters not a jot.
> A youth is dead who might have been alive
> Had the Defendant found him means to thrive,
> Lodg'd him in Strawberry Hill in decent dress
> And made him the Corrector of his Press.
> Why did he not – His reason, I repeat
> Only because he thought the Youth a Cheat.

Other supporters, strangely enough, included the pro-Rowleyites, Bryant and Milles. They defended him as they would any other member of their class. Chatterton, wrote Bryant, who had been at Eton with Walpole, had 'fallen very cruelly upon a person whose rank and character deserved far greater respect'. Milles echoed this view, and the point was carried still further when the first biography of Chatterton appeared in the *Biographia Britannica* in 1789. It was not surprising, said the author, Doctor Gregory, that Walpole had ignored a young man 'whose birth and education entitled him to no high pretensions . . . it was a degree of special condescension to take any notice whatever of the matter'.

Gregory's account of Walpole's relations with Chatterton (which Walpole himself had read before publication) was extremely favourable. It would be the highest degree of absurdity, he wrote, to accuse Walpole of causing Chatterton's death.

Here, if Walpole had been wise, he should have let his defence rest. But criticism had made him hypersensitive. Later that year, Barrett's long-waited *History of Bristol* at last made its appearance – he had been spurred on to finish it, he explained in his preface, by Doctor Glynn, Bryant's Rowleyite colleague, who had warned him, in Latin, to keep mortality before his eyes. In the *History* Chatterton's letters to Walpole were published for the first time, attached to a commentary on Rowley's poems. Walpole by then was seventy-two – it was twenty years since his correspondence with Chatterton; perhaps he was growing confused and was genuinely mistaken, perhaps he simply lost his nerve. He denied that he had ever received the letters. There was an immediate outcry: the letters, as Barrett could show, were postmarked, moreover Walpole had already admitted receiving them in his printed explanation ten years earlier. The resulting confusion and the imputation of cowardice in his denials did more to tarnish his reputation than any previous statement. For the rest of his life Chatterton remained a source of pain and embarrassment. 'I remarked', said one commentator, 'that Lord Orford dwelt upon his conduct about Chatterton more than any other subject, and that to all literary commentators.'

As for Barrett, the appearance of his *History* brought him little joy. Its credibility diminished by the reliance placed on the writings of the 'gode preeste Thomas Rowlie' and architectural drawings from the same source, his life-work was greeted with derision. He died a year later. 'I am sorry, very sorry,' wrote Horace Walpole to Hannah More in Bristol, 'for what you tell me about Barrett's fate. Though he did write worse than Shakespeare, it was a great pity he was told so as it killed him.'

Walpole's dismissal of Chatterton was a tragically lost opportunity; and it is hard to absolve him of snobbery at the least. But he paid a bitter price for his neglect – while Dodsley, who had not even replied to Chatterton's applications – escaped without a breath of criticism. The fact was that Walpole, son of a prime minister, heir to an earldom, creator of Strawberry Hill, was far more newsworthy than Dodsley – or for that matter Chatterton himself. Without the lustre of Walpole's reputation Chatterton, for all the interest aroused by his poems, might have faded into obscurity. The Romantic Movement caught up with him while his name, thanks to Walpole, was on everybody's lips; the transition to romantic hero followed naturally.

Part III   Legend

8 'Love and Madness'

Nature had infused too strong a proportion of passion into Werther's composition; his feelings, like those of our own Chatterton, were too intense to support the load of accumulated distress; and like him his diapason ended in death.

Translator's introduction: *Sorrows of Werther* (1779)

Horace Walpole, by his supposed neglect, had sown the first seeds of the Chatterton myth. They fell on propitious ground. The Romantic Movement was beginning to stir. While the literary world continued to argue over the authorship of the Rowley poems the public, uninterested in antiquarian niceties, had decided the matter in favour of Chatterton. Forgery and neglected genius were more exciting than medieval glossaries, Rowley the monk, a cowled figure in the manner of a Gothic novel, no more than a fashionable decoration. While Chatterton's detractors in the debate continued to harp on his low morals and lack of principle, the popular picture of his character was summed up in James Beattie's 'The Minstrel or the Progress of Genius':

> And yet poor Edwin was no vulgar boy,
> Deep thought oft seem'd to fix his infant eye.
> Dainties he heeded not, nor gaude, nor toy,
> Save one short pipe of rudest minstrelsy:
> Silent when glad; affectionate, though shy;
> And now his look was most demurely sad;
> And now he laugh'd aloud yet none knew why.
> The neighbours stared and sigh'd yet bless'd the lad
> Some deem'd him wondrous wise and some believ'd
>   him mad.

A host of sentimental poems bewailed his fate, Chatterton's youth and lowly origins offering hopes of fame, not necessarily posthumous, to many an apprentice with literary leanings. His deathbed became a standard theme in prints and engravings. Chatterton handkerchiefs, printed in red or blue, depicted the distressed poet in his garret, the accompanying text giving the key to his appeal: 'His destiny, cruel as it was, gives a charm to his verses.'

In Bristol, a commemorative concert was given in the assembly rooms, with music and an ode specially composed for the occasion, the programme decorated with a picture of 'Genius conducting Chatterton in the habit of a Bluecoat Boy to her Altar'; and Mr Philip Thicknesse, a gentleman living near Bath, erected a ruined monument to Chatterton – a Gothic arch entwined with laurel, set between the bosom of two hills – where he could mourn the fate of unrecognized genius in solitude.

Meanwhile Goethe's *Sorrows of Werther*, over which Europe was swooning, had set the seal on the idea of romantic suicide. Like Werther's, Chatterton's suicide could be seen as the gesture of one whose sufferings were more intense, because his sensibilities were finer, than those of coarser mortals. Nature had anticipated art: Werther had been published four years after Chatterton's death.

The idea of Chatterton as the victim of Wertherian passions was taken up in *Love and Madness*, a best-selling novel, which more than any other single work established him as a romantic hero. Its author, Herbert Croft, later a respectable baronet and clergyman, but then an impecunious literary adventurer, having made his own researches into Chatterton's life, proceeded to weave them into a real-life story as sensational as, and strongly influenced by, the tale of Werther and Charlotte. Written in letter form, *Love and Madness* was based on a correspondence retrieved from the condemned cell of James Hackman, executed in 1779. Hackman, a clergyman distracted by jealousy, had murdered the singer Martha Reay, mistress of the Earl of Sandwich, intending, but failing, to kill himself with a second shot. A copy of Werther's last letter to Charlotte had been found on the ground by the pistol.

As was often the custom in the eighteenth century, Hackman

had kept copies of his own letters, and these, combined with Miss Reay's, were published by Croft within a year of the murder, the intriguing subtitle – 'A Story Too True' – and the thin disguise of initials in place of proper names making their origins obvious.

The story was dramatic enough to need no heightening, but Sir Herbert did not mean to waste his Chatterton material, whose sensational character could only enhance his theme. The correspondence bore the marks of heavy editing. Through it all ran anecdotes of suicide, murder and executions, presages that would seem more striking had Sir Herbert's influence been less apparent. They culminated in the section on Chatterton, a hundred pages (over a third of the book) of his own researches, interpolated so skilfully that the marks of scissors and paste were scarcely visible. Only ten years had passed since the poet's death and Sir Herbert's findings were based on the still vivid memories of those who had known him. The topical interest of this, combined with the drama of Miss Reay, her lover and Lord Sandwich, ensured the success of the book, which ran through seven editions.

Lord Sandwich, who appeared as Lord S. in the book, was First Lord of the Admiralty, extremely unpopular and universally known as 'Jemmy Twitcher'. He had earned his nickname when, 'in tones of more hypocrisy than would have been tolerable in a professed Methodist' he had tried to throw mud on his erstwhile drinking companion Wilkes; during Wilkes's prosecution by Parliament he had read out, to his fellow members of the House of Lords, obscenely libellous verses which Wilkes had composed and given him. This treachery rebounded. At *The Beggar's Opera*, given in his presence a few nights later, Macheath's remark – 'that Jemmy Twitcher should peach me I own surprises me' – brought a roar of recognition from the audience. The nickname stuck for ever after.

But despite political cynicism, arrogance and a rakish past, there was a softer side to Jemmy Twitcher, which revealed itself in his long-standing attachment to the singer Martha Reay – M. in *Love and Madness*. He was separated from his wife and for thirteen years Miss Reay had presided over his household in London and at Hinchinbrooke, his rambling Tudor house in Huntingdon. She had

F

borne him nine children, three of them living. At musical evenings she would sing in a soprano voice of great beauty, and could play the harpsichord brilliantly. The concerts at Hinchinbrooke were famous. Though it was understood that she would not join in the conversation when ladies of rank were present, she took her place at table and in the drawing room. Her talents had brought her offers from Covent Garden, but she refused all inducements; she had come from a background of slums and despite her ambiguous position was grateful for her present security, and was bound by affection, if not love, to her protector, who was twenty years her senior. Her portrait by Dance shows a gentle oval face, comely rather than pretty, piled-up dark hair, a slender figure, a book of music on her taffeta lap.

One evening two young officers, stationed nearby, were invited to Hinchinbrooke. One of them was James Hackman – H. in *Love and Madness*. He was twenty, Martha Reay was thirty-three. They fell in love and before long became lovers, meeting both at the Admiralty and at Hinchinbrooke, where Lord Sandwich, unsuspecting and pleased to find company in the country, was a polished host. But Hackman was penniless, and Martha Reay feared for the future of her children should Lord Sandwich's support be withdrawn. She dared not leave her protector, despite Hackman's frantic proposals of marriage. For all her ardour she felt bound too by loyalty to one who had supported her for so many years.

> I gang like a ghost and I do not care to spin
> I fain would think on Jamie but that would be a
>   sin;
> I must e'en do my best a good wife to be,
> For auld Robin Grey has been kind to me.

'Your name is also Jamie,' she wrote, transcribing the ballad to her lover. 'I wept like an infant over it this morning.'

Hackman was offered promotion and the chance of a transfer to Ireland. It is possible that Lord Sandwich, catching wind of the affair, had discreetly arranged his removal. Martha Reay besought him to accept the offer: 'Go, I conjure you, go! . . . Either stay and let our affection discover and ruin us – or go. On the bended knees of love I intreat you H., my dearest H., to go.'

For two years the pair corresponded, resolving on Miss Reay's insistence to write only on matters of general interest. Hence the letters contained a mixture of poetry, anecdote and literary chit-chat, and finally, with an artful transition from genuine to false, Sir Herbert interpolated the central section on Chatterton. 'The task you have set me about Chatterton is only a further proof of your regard for me,' he wrote in the guise of H. 'You know the warmth of my passions and you think if I do not employ myself they may flame up and consume me. Well then, I will spend a morning or two in arranging what I have collected in respect of the author of Rowley's poems.'

Thereafter followed the fruit of Croft's own researches and conclusions on Chatterton, conclusions which did much to establish his legend. He likened him to Apollo reincarnated, compared him at length to Milton – to Milton's disadvantage; and asserted 'that an army of Macedonian and Swedish mad butchers ran before him', meaning presumably the youthful Alexander the Great and Charles XII. Hyperbole indeed, but Chatterton could always inspire exaggerated reactions.

He scoffed at the scholars who maintained the poems to be fifteenth-century. 'Did you start when I wrote "the author of Rowley's poems"?' he asked Miss Reay. 'My mind does not now harbour a doubt that Chatterton wrote the whole, whatever I thought when we read them together at H[inchinbrooke].'

He made a spirited defence of Chatterton against the charge of forgery (an offence no greater than his own manipulations of fact and fiction). Chatterton's greatest fault, he said, was his poverty. The deceptions of Walpole and Ossian had been greeted with nothing but praise:

Suffer me to ask what the prudery of our critics would have said had the 'Song to Aella' been produced by Mr Warton's nephew or by a relation of Mr Walpole? The sins of the forgery and the impostor would then have been boasted by the child's most distant relations. . . . 'When a rich man speaketh' says the son of Shirach, 'every man holdeth his tongue; and lo! what he says is extolled to the clouds: but if a poor man speak, they say "what fellow is this" ' . . .

Chatterton's self-imposed secrecy, he went on, was perhaps the most wonderful part of his deception:

Let any man, at any time of his life, make an experiment of not communicating to a single individual a single scheme, a single prospect, a single circumstance regarding himself. . . . There are easier tasks. This boy did that during his entire life.

He grew indignant about the accusations of profligacy cast at Chatterton, culminating in the statement of one learned antiquarian that Chatterton's death was of little consequence since he could not long have escaped hanging:

Do *profligate* and *unprincipled*, some of the tenderest epithets vouchsafed unto poor Chatterton, mean dishonest or undutiful, an unkind brother or an unfeeling child? The dullest enemies of his genius can produce no evidence of any such crime. . . . Do they mean that, being a young man, he was addicted to women, like all youths of strong imaginations? Do the epithets mean that he exhibited those damnable proofs of his crimes which Bouganville exported into the country of Omiah? The proofs (if there were any, which his bedfellow at his first lodging in town denies) only show that he was unlucky. . . .

He described the treatment of Chatterton's mother and sister, so often attacked and pestered by enquirers that they 'might easily have been made to believe that injured Justice demanded their lives at Tyburn, for being the mother and sister of him who was suspected to have *forged* the poems of Rowley'. As for Catcott and Barrett, both of whom had made large sums from the sale of the Chatterton manuscripts, Mrs Chatterton 'acknowledges to have received the immense sum of five guineas from the hand of Mr Catcott; and Mr Barrett, without fee, cured the whitlowed finger of the sister'.

'Mr Croft has scandalously abused me in "Love and Madness",' wrote Catcott when he read this, to Dean Milles. Croft, he complained, had called on him in the course of his researches, when – 'though his sentiments are now extremely different' – he had confessed himself convinced by Catcott's arguments for the existence of Rowley, and bestowed encomiums on his scholarship. He had tried to persuade Catcott to let him take a copy of

Chatterton's poem 'The Exhibition', in which 'almost all the Clergy of the town, many Medical Gentlemen and Myself are very scandalously and indecently satirized'. Mercifully, said Catcott, he had not let himself be persuaded; if he had, he did not doubt, despite Croft's solemn assurances to the contrary, that it would have been printed in *Love and Madness*. Dean Milles, snobbish as ever, was surprised by Croft's behaviour and defence of Chatterton. Mr Croft had married the niece of a friend of his, a Miss Burchier Cleeve, niece of Lady Young, who on his death 'will inherit a very considerable Fortune'.

From Chatterton's sister Croft obtained a memorandum of her brother. 'Conscious of my inabilities to write to a man of letters,' she gave her recollections of his childhood:

My brother very early discovered a thirst for preheminence, I remember before he was 5 years old he would always preside over his playmates as their master and they his hired servants. . . . He was a lover of truth from the earlyest dawn of reason, and nothing would move him so much as being bely'd. When in the school we were informed by the usher, his master depended upon his verasity on all occasions.

This statement by Chatterton's sister was taken up, after the publication of *Love and Madness*, by the pro-Rowley faction; Chatterton's love of truth, they said, would have made it impossible for him to lie when claiming that the poems were medieval. Later, she went on,

. . . he would often speak in great raptures of the undoubted success of his plans for future life. He was introduced to Mr Barrett, Mr Catcott, his ambition increased daily. His spirits was rather uneven, sometimes so gloom'd that for many days together he would say very little and that by constraint. At other times exceeding cheerful. . . . He found he studied best towards the full of the moon and would often sit up all night and write by moonlight. . . . He began to be universally known among the young men. He had many cap acquaintances but I am confident few intimates. . . . He would frequently walk the College Green with the young girls that statedly walked there to parade their finery. But I readily believe he was no debauchee (tho' some have reported it). . . .

More important than his sister's reminiscences, and indeed the principal source of information on Chatterton's stay in London, apart from Croft's interviews with his landlord and cousin, were the letters which Chatterton had sent home to his family; here Croft, behaving worse than the enquirers he had criticized, took disgraceful advantage of Chatterton's relations. An ingratiating stranger, he had called on Mrs Chatterton and her daughter and persuaded them to lend him their letters 'for an hour' – his emotion, he said, would be too great should he read them in their presence. Instead, he did not return them for several months; and on the publication of *Love and Madness* the horrified pair saw their private letters included in the sensational narrative. Mrs Chatterton went into 'strong hystericks' and was heard to affirm, said Catcott, that nothing since the death of her son had occasioned her so much distress.

The first letter was written the day after his arrival:

Here I am safe and in high spirits – To give you a journal of my tour would not be unneccessary. After riding in the basket to Bridlington, I mounted the top of the coach and rid easy and agreeably entertained by the conversation of a quaker *in dress* but little so in personals and behaviour. . . . I left him in Bath, when finding it rained pretty fast, I entered an inside passenger to Speenhamland, the half way stage, paying seven shillings; t'was lucky I did so, for it snowed all night, and on the Marlborough downs the snow was near a foot high.

At seven in the morning I breakfasted at Speenhamland and then mounted the coach box for the remainder of the day, which was a remarkable fine one. – Honest gee ho complimented me with assuring me that I sat bolder and tighter than any person who ever rid with him. . . .

Got into London about 5 o'clock in the evening – called upon Mr Edmunds, Mr Fell, Mr Hamilton. . . . Great encouragement from them; all approve of my design; shall soon be settled . . . Seen all aunts, cousins – all well – and I am welcome . . . Sister, grandmother, &c. &c. &c. remembered. – I remain,

> Your dutiful son,
> T. Chatterton

In his next letter he exclaimed with satisfaction:

Good God! how superior is London to that despicable place Bristol – here is none of your little meannesses, none of your mercenary securities which disgrace that miserable Hamlet. . . .

And in another, headed 'Tom's Coffee House':

Dear sister, There is such a noise of business and politicks, in the room that my inaccuracy in writing to you is highly excusable. My present profession obliges me to frequent places of the best resort. To begin with, what every female conversation begins with, dress. I employ my money now into fitting myself fashionably and getting into good company: this last article always brings me in interest. . . . If money flowed in as fast as honours, I would give you a portion of £5000.

From the King's Bench prison he wrote with bravado,

Don't be alarmed at the name of this place. I am not here as a prisoner. Matters go on swimmingly: Mr Fell having offended certain persons, they have set his creditors upon him, and he is safe in Kings Bench. . . . Last week, being in the pit of Drury Lane Theatre, I contracted an immediate acquaintance (which you know is no hard task to me) with a young gentleman in Cheapside, partner in a music shop, the greatest in the city. Hearing I could write he desired me to write a few songs for him, this I did the same night and conveyed them to him next morning. These he showed to a doctor in music, and I am invited to treat with this doctor on the footing of a composer, for Ranelagh and the Gardens. *Bravo, hey boys, up we go!*

There were also messages to girls,

My sister will remember me to Miss Sandford. I have not quite forgot her; though there are so many pretty milliners & c. that I have quite forgot myself – Miss Rumsey, if she comes to London, would do well as an old acquaintance to send me her address. London is not Bristol – we may patrol the town for a day, without raising one whisper or nod of scandal: if she refuses may the curse of all antiquated virgins falls on her. . . .

The tone of coxcomb-like jauntiness never wore thin. His last letter kept up the pretence:

I have an universal acquaintance; my company is courted everywhere; and could I humble myself to go into a compter, could have

twenty places before now; but I must be among the great. State matters
suit me better than commercial. The ladies are not out of my acquaintance. I have a deal of business now, and must therefore bid you adieu.

Four days later he was dead. Croft paid a visit to the room where
his body was found:

It was half an hour of the most exquisite sensations. My visit of
devotion was paid in the morning I remember; but I was not myself
again all day. To look round the room; to say to myself, here stood
his bed; there the poison was set; in that window he loitered for some
hours before he retired to his last rest, envying the meanest passengers
and wishing he could exchange his own feelings and intellects, for their
manual powers and abilities. Then abhorrence of his death, abhorrence
of the world, and I know not how many different and contradictory,
but all distracting, ideas! Nothing could tempt me to undergo another
such half hour.

But the drama of Hackman and Reay was reaching its own climax. After nearly two years absence in Ireland Hackman received
the offer of a parsonage and a good living in England, should he
take holy orders. He sold out of the army and became a clergyman. The physical obstacles to their marriage seemed at last
overcome; there was income enough to support a wife and children. But faced with the realities of choice Martha Reay faltered.
A romantic attachment was one thing, but she feared the tremen-
dous step of breaking with Lord Sandwich and starting a new life
at thirty-five. Lord Sandwich, on his part, sensing a threat to his
domestic peace, took discreet steps to put an end to the affair.
At his instigation Signora Galli, Martha Reay's duenna and singing
mistress, called on Hackman to point out the difficulties of the
match. Her reasonings had no effect, Hackman persisted more
fervently. Signora Galli resorted to stratagem, in Italian opera
style. She hinted, untruthfully, that Martha Reay had taken a new
lover, that she no longer cared for him. Hackman, too shattered
to question her statement, was beside himself with anguish. There
was no future but suicide. He determined to kill himself and die
at the feet of his perfidious mistress. Taking a pair of pistols, he
lay in wait for her outside the Covent Garden opera house. As

she came out and was stepping into her coach, he rushed up to her, and on an impulse shot twice, killing her, but merely wounding himself in the temple. He lay in the gutter, too weak to despatch himself with the butt of his pistol, moaning, 'Kill me, kill me' to the horrified bystanders.

At his trial his appearance in the dock, with a circle of black sticking-plaster on his forehead, aroused a murmur of sympathy in the crowded courtroom. He pleaded not guilty, not as he explained to escape punishment, but in order that he should not a second time be accessory to the sin of attempting his own life. As he lay in the condemned cell at Newgate a letter was delivered: 'If the murderer of Miss . . . wishes to live, the man he has most injured will do his utmost to procure his life.' It was from Lord Sandwich.

Hackman refused his help. He wished to die, not live. He had only one request: 'Could he be pardoned in the world by the man he has most injured – Oh my Lord, when I meet her in another world enable me to tell her (if departed spirits are ignorant of such things) that you forgive us both, that you will be a father to her dear infants.' Lord Sandwich needed no such prompting. Martha Reay's children were handsomely looked after. He himself was heartbroken – immune to his political unpopularity, which, with corruption at the Admiralty a public scandal, was at its height, he had broken down at the news of her death. 'His Lordship's sensations expressed the greatest agonies,' said one newspaper, 'and what ever may be his sentiments in political matters, in this affair he has shown a tenderness which does the highest credit to his heart.'

Hackman's hanging was attended by large crowds, among them that connoisseur of executions, Boswell. Another spectator, the younger Angelo, recounted his visit to the Surgeons' Hall, where the body was being dissected for medical research, as was the custom after hanging: 'On leaving the place we retired to Dolly's Chop House. Our first dish was *pork* chops and the sight I had witnessed produced such an impression that not only did I reject them in disgust but I have never been able to eat them since.'

Horace Walpole, who had described the case with gossipy

relish in a letter to the Countess of Upper Ossory, was less amused, when Croft's bestseller appeared, to find his own name linked with *Love and Madness*. 'You may wonder how *I* should be dragged into this correspondence who never saw either of the lovers in my days,' he wrote. It was of course in connection with Chatterton. 'I am acquitted of being accessory to Chatterton's death, which is gracious; but much blamed for speaking of his bad character and for being too hard on his forgeries. . . .' There was no point, he felt, in restating his case. 'Blunder I see people will and talk of what they do not understand, and what care I?' and so with an airiness, perhaps assumed, moved on to another topic.

9 The Shakespeare Forgeries

Comfort and joy's forever fled
He ne'er will warble more!
Ah me! the sweetest youth is dead
That e'er tun'd reed before.
The Hand of Mis'ry bowed him low,
E'en Hope forsook his brain;
Relentless man contemn'd his woe:
To you he sigh'd in vain.
Oppressed with want, in wild despair he cried
'No more I'll live', swallowed the draught and
died.

WILLIAM HENRY IRELAND: acrostic on Chatterton

Among the subscribers to *Love and Madness* there had been few
more eager readers than the family of Samuel Ireland, a former
silk-weaver from Spitalfields. Now comfortably off, he lived in
London, where he dealt in paintings and engravings, often of
views depicted by himself, and amassed a collection of rare books
and curious objects – ranging from a velvet purse presented by
Henry VIII to Anne Boleyn to a silver fruit-knife which had
belonged to Joseph Addison. His passion above all was Shakespeare and he was assiduous in his pursuit of Shakespearean relics,
whilst his conversation was spiced with quotations from his
works. (Shakespeare, having gone through a period of decline in
the early part of the century, was now high in favour, with
Garrick's performances setting the seal on Shakespeare worship.)

The story of *Love and Madness* was not without piquancy for
Samuel Ireland, since his mistress, Mrs Freeman, who presided
over the household, included the Earl of Sandwich among her
former lovers. But for his youngest child, William Henry, it was
the section on Chatterton which made the deepest impression.

He was a romantic youth, just seventeen, who had dreamed over Chaucer, Percy's *Reliques* and *The Castle of Otranto*:

I have often sighed to be the inmate of some gloomy castle, or that having lost my way upon a dreary heath, I might like Sir Bertram, have been conducted to some enchanted mansion. Sometimes I have wished that by the distant chime of a bell I had found the hospitable porch of some old monastery where, with the holy brotherhood, having shared at the board their homely fare I might have afterwards enjoyed upon a pallet a sound repose, and with their blessing the ensuing morn have hied me in pursuit of fresh adventures.

Now the story of Chatterton, as recounted by Sir Herbert Croft, fired his imagination so strongly that he found himself desiring 'nothing so ardently as the termination of my existence in a similar cause'. He was deeply struck by the parallels between himself and the unhappy poet. Like him he was seventeen and indentured to a lawyer, a position he found no more congenial than Chatterton had done. Like him he yearned for recognition – Chatterton had sought it from the world at large, but for William Henry his own father's appreciation meant still more than fame. For Samuel Ireland had little good to say for his son, whom he considered a dunce and a disappointment; it was William Henry's pathetic desire to impress his father that was to land him in such trouble.

He brooded on his affinities with Chatterton. He composed an acrostic on his name, and, more importantly, imitations of his medieval poetry. Forgery seemed the logical next step. With Chatterton's example in mind he purchased a quarto tract of prayers, dedicated to Queen Elizabeth, with the intention of forging a covering note which would establish it as an autograph copy from its author to the Queen herself. His first attempt, in watered-down ink, was not convincing; but a friendly bookseller presented him with a bottle of ink used for marbling book covers, which being pale and brownish had a more authentic appearance. The tract, with the note slipped between the vellum cover and the paper, was presented to his father. Samuel Ireland examined it with a collector's zeal, and his praise and delight were balm to his son's soul.

Gratified by the ease of this deception, William Henry became more ambitious. Before long he presented his father who had often declared he would willingly sacrifice his entire library for a scrap of Shakespeare's writing, with the actual signature of the bard, attached to the foot of an ancient lease, and sealed with two undoubtedly genuine seals. The signature had been traced from a facsimile, the parchment cut from an old rent-roll in his master's chambers and the seals, which had come from the same source, had been split open with a hot knife and reattached with new wax at the back, then sooted over.

To his father's eager enquiries, William Henry replied that he had discovered the deed in an ancient chest of manuscripts stored in the attic of a gentleman, who wished to remain anonymous, but being indebted to William Henry over a claim to a legacy, had given him permission to take what he liked from his papers. Nobody questioned this improbable story and the authenticity of the signature was felt to be further established when the seals were remarked to represent a quintain or tilting target – an unplanned coincidence. The play on words between this and 'Shake-speer' seemed conclusive to the experts called in to examine the find.

William Henry became still bolder. Shakespeare's signature had gone unquestioned; now he would try a whole letter in his writing. Since scholars had often surmised that Shakespeare showed sympathies towards the Church of Rome (particularly on account of references made to purgatory by the ghost in *Hamlet*), he decided to vindicate him by showing him to have been firmly of the Protestant persuasion. He produced a Confession of Faith, a ridiculous document, for whose spelling Chatterton, alas, provided the example. It ended fervently, 'O cherishe usse like the sweete Chickenne thatte under the coverte offe herre spread-ynge Wings Receyves herre lyttle Broode . . .' and was signed, with the ease of careful practice, 'Wm. Shakespeare'.

When the learned divine Doctor Parr, having listened to a sonorous reading of the document by Samuel Ireland, burst out, saying, 'Sir, we have very fine passages in our church service, and our litany abounds with beauties; but here, sir, is a man who has outdistanced us all!' it is hardly surprising that William Henry could scarcely believe his ears, or that from then on his forgeries grew more and more reckless.

In quick succession he presented the world with a love letter to Anne Hathaway, a lock of Shakespeare's hair, a self-portrait, letters, playbills and poems, using for parchment, as Chatterton had done, pieces cut off the foot of ancient legal deeds. A new version of Shakespeare's Last Will and Testament even included a legacy to his friend William Henry Ireland, who had once saved him from drowning. Could this be an ancestor of the Ireland family, nay more, was he, could he possibly be, the mysterious Mr W.H. of the sonnets?

Samuel Ireland was beside himself with delight. Worshippers of Shakespeare flocked to his house to see the precious manuscripts, where he presided on his Shakespeare chair which he had purchased from the owners of Anne Hathaway's cottage. 'To see their settled physiognomies,' wrote William Henry in his *Confessions*, 'frequently aroused in me a desire for laughter which it has required every effort on my part to restrain.' Boswell, that indefatigable curiosity-hunter, was among the visitors. After examining the documents carefully, and discoursing on the internal as well as the external proofs of their validity, he called for brandy and water, and having downed it he rose from his chair, saying, 'Well; I shall now die contented, since I have lived to witness the present day.' Then, kneeling down in front of the volume containing the papers, he continued, 'I now kiss the invaluable relics of our bard; and thanks to God that I have lived to see them.'

Not all the visitors were so convinced, though there was an impressive number of scholars among the believers, and the Duke of Clarence added his royal support. But there were menacing rumblings from the greatest Shakespeare expert of the day, Edmond Malone. Twelve years earlier he had been among the first to unmask Chatterton's Rowley poems as forgeries. Now, with equally well-based scepticism, he questioned the authenticity of the Ireland papers. The *Morning Telegraph*, too, was inclined to spoof the affair, with a message from Shakespeare to Ben Jonson: 'Deeree Sirree, Wille youe doee meee thee favvourree too dinnee wythee mee onnn Friddaye nextte attt twoo off theee clockee too eatee sommee muttonne choppes and somme poottaattooeesse . . .'

Meanwhile Samuel Ireland, still convinced by his son's discoveries, was waiting for the crowning piece of all – *Vortigern and Rowena*, a hitherto unknown play by Shakespeare. This, William Henry informed him, he had just unearthed among the papers of his unknown friend – who shunned the limelight, despite all demands that he should come forward. Since the friend did not wish to part with the original (at which we need not wonder, since the feat of forging five acts as well as composing them would have been great indeed), William Henry was in the process of transcribing it.

Despite bids from Covent Garden it was arranged that Sheridan should have the privilege of presenting the new play at Drury Lane, and that the great Shakespearean actor John Philip Kemble should take the title role.

Time was short. Frenziedly William Henry worked at *Vortigern* in the intervals of his work at the attorney's office. His story was taken from Holinshed's *Chronicles*, an impeccable source, which he had found in his father's library. It was a Saxon tragedy, with Hengist and Horsus as minor characters and a complicated plot of murder, incest and ambition. In order that the Shakespearean form should be followed he counted every line of one of his plays (his *Confessions* do not say which) and kept to the same length in his own. Alas, he had chosen one of Shakespeare's longest plays, and when Sheridan was presented with the final copy he remarked that the purchase of the play was at any rate a good one, as there were two plays and a half instead of one.

Vortigern was finished in two months, but in the interval Sheridan showed signs of getting cold feet. The unbelievers were gathering their forces, early supporters were having second thoughts, and skits were appearing almost daily in the press. As for Sheridan, the more he read of the play the more dubious he became. Putting down the manuscript he observed thoughtfully: 'There are certainly some bold ideas but very crude and indigested. It is very odd; one would be led to think that Shakespeare must have been very young when he wrote the play.' Nevertheless an agreement was signed between him and Samuel Ireland, with a down-payment of £300, of which William Henry received £60, his first and only profit out of the whole affair.

Rehearsals got under way slowly. Public scepticism was growing, and a pamphlet by Malone condemning the papers as forgeries was at the printers and soon to be published. Mrs Siddons, who was to have played the part of Rowena, developed a convenient illness and withdrew from the cast, and Kemble, her brother, who was manager as well as actor at Drury Lane, announced his intention of putting on the first performance on April Fools' Day.

This dastardly plan was foiled and the first night was in fact on 2 April 1796. Two days before, Malone's pamphlet, totally damning, was published, to the confusion of the Irelands and the pro-Shakespearean party. *Vortigern* therefore took on the status of a test case, and every seat in the theatre was sold out, as the cynical Sheridan had foreseen. Public curiosity would certainly fill the house for the night, even at inflated prices, for, 'you know,' said Sheridan to Kemble, 'every Englishman considers himself as good a judge of Shakespeare as of his pint of porter.'

On the first night the Duke of Clarence, with Mrs Jordan, was in the royal box; Samuel Ireland and Mrs Freeman, with an air of aggrieved importance, were seated conspicuously near by. William Henry, whose state of nerves can be imagined, watched from behind the scenes, his heart in his mouth. The prologue stated the case,

> No common cause your verdict now demands,
> Before the court immortal Shakespeare stands.

The first two acts went fairly well with polite attention from the audience. The trouble started in the third, when the treble voice of a minor actor had the audience in fits of laughter, but worse was to come with the death of Horsus in the fourth. The part was played by a Mr Philimore, 'of large-nosed memory'. Stricken by the deadly blow, he fell, but 'so placed his unfortunate carcase that on the falling of the drop curtain he was literally divided between the audience and his brethren of the sock and buskin'. Groaning beneath the weight he struggled to extricate himself, 'which for a dead man was something in the style of Mr Bannister jun. in "The Critic" who tells Mr Puff that he "cannot stay there *dying* all day".'

The evening ended in howls of execration, with the actors guying their parts and oranges pelted on the believers. Thereafter the great Shakespearean manuscripts were hopelessly discredited. The imposture, said the critics, outdistanced even Chatterton's in impudence.

Samuel Ireland refused to accept the critics' verdict. William Henry's pathetic hopes that he would be welcomed as a prodigy, a second Chatterton, by his father were in vain. To his dying day he continued to believe the papers genuine, not least because he considered his offspring too stupid to write anything that could be mistaken for Shakespeare's. He stuck to his views through thick and thin, maintaining them in pamphlets and refuting those of his son; for William Henry, once he saw the game was up, quickly cut his losses, confessed all publicly, and though sometimes in dire straits for money was able to support himself as a journalist and writer on the strength of his fame as a forger. In 1805 he published his *Confessions*, recounting the whole story and, more on the grounds of genius than of forgery, comparing himself to Chatterton.

He had been to Bristol to visit the haunts of his spiritual brother shortly before, and was able to recount his experience in the *Confessions*. St Mary Redcliffe and the chests in the muniments room were naturally his first port of call; next he had called on Chatterton's sister, Mrs Newton where he asked her for anecdotes of her brother:

'Do you call to mind circumstances of a particular nature respecting your brother when he was a child?'

'He was always very reserved and fond of seclusion; we often missed him for half a day together; and once I well remember his being most severely chastised for a long absence; at which however he did not shed one tear but merely said "it was hard indeed to be whipt for reading".'

She then proceeded to acquaint me that some malevolent aspersions had been thrown out as to his moral character, and particularly his

G

being partial to abandoned women, which she positively denied, with tears in her eyes.

At a bookseller in a nearby street William Henry got into conversation about Chatterton who, he discovered, had been in the habit of frequenting the shop after school-hours. Too poor to make purchases, he had been allowed to peruse the shelves. 'He was never communicative, merely bowing his head as he entered the shop and making a similar obeisance on retiring.'

On the same visit Joseph Cottle, the Bristol publisher, who with the help of Southey was preparing a collected edition of Chatterton's work, invited him to insert a sample of his forging ability at the end of a copy-book of Chatterton's which he had obtained from Barrett. Ireland felt flattered indeed.

For the rest of his life he continued to glory in his affinities with Chatterton:

> Farewell, sweet youth! One bosom still can melt,
> Still gaze with anguish and thy woes deplore;
> Still vainly soothe the sufferings thou hast felt
> Those agonies which thou canst feel no more.

His own sensibilities, he implied, were equally delicate.

A book of poems entitled *Neglected Genius* was almost entirely devoted to Chatterton; in order to demonstrate that Chatterton's medieval poems could easily have been written by a modern writer – 'since there are still some individuals at Bristol willing to attribute Chatterton's productions to the supposed Rowley' – he applied his old skills to creating his own version of a Rowley poem. Its refrain:

> The poyntelle's glowe
> Lyes cale belowe
> All nethe the cypress tree,

bore a close resemblance to the song in *Aella*. 'Poyntelle,' noted Ireland in a footnote, 'is the old English word for poet.'

Delusions of talent and memories of his early success buoyed him up through a life of vicissitudes, and he was able always to contemplate with satisfaction the association, as he expressed it, between 'the Rowliean Chatterton and the Shakespearean Ireland, whose memories will live as long as old chests and old manuscripts stand on record'.

10 The Poet's Poet: Coleridge and Southey

> O Chatterton! that thou wert yet alive!
> Sure thou would'st spread the canvass to the gale,
> And love with us the tinkling team to drive
> O'er peaceful Freedom's undivided dale;
> And we, at sober eve, would round thee throng
> Hanging, enraptured, on thy stately song!
> And greet with smiles the young-eyed Poesy
> All deftly masked as hoar Antiquity.
>
> SAMUEL TAYLOR COLERIDGE:
> 'Monody on the Death of Chatterton' (1796)

In the years immediately following Chatterton's death, though the Rowley poems had been the subject of passionate discussion, their greatest interest had seemed to lie in the question of their date and authorship. Their beauty and originality, despite the lip-service paid to them, had been of secondary importance. But thanks to the publicity surrounding the Rowley controversy, and later to the development of Chatterton's image as a martyred genius, the poems remained in print. Thus, almost inevitably, the early reading of the Romantic poets in the generation following his included Chatterton's work; and as they grew up his literary influence, latent for over twenty years, began to make itself felt.

To the Romantic poets, Chatterton was a portent, whose poetry, with its return to the Gothic past, heralded their own reaction against the classicism of the Age of Reason; while in the prosodic sphere it foreshadowed the overthrow of the rigid verse forms – the Popeian couplet above all – of the eighteenth century.

The slur of forgery no longer applied. In the Romantic view Chatterton's claim that his poems were medieval was no more than the assertion of an imaginative truth. 'I believe Macpherson

and Chatterton that what they say is ancient is so,' wrote Blake.
Blake, seven years younger than Chatterton, grew up knowing
his poetry; Chatterton, with Shakespeare, Milton and the Bible,
was among the favourite studies of his early days. In both the
love of Gothic architecture, inspired in Blake's case by his studies
as an engraver's apprentice in Westminster Abbey, became a
ruling passion; and Chatterton, however tentatively, had first
sounded the note of lyric freedom which Blake would bring to
English poetry. There are occasional echoes of Chatterton in
Blake's work: the relationship, noted by Rossetti, between
Chatterton's 'Flattery's a cloak and I will put it on' and Blake's
image 'Innocence is a winter's gown'; the song from *An Island in
the Moon*,

> When old Corruption first begun
> Adorned in yellow vest

recalling Chatterton's chorus from 'Goddwyn':

> When Freedom dreste, yn blodde steyned veste.

An Island in the Moon itself, Blake's unfinished satire, is scattered
with references to Chatterton and the Rowley controversy. 'In
the first place,' remarks one character, apropos of Chatterton's
fate,

> I think, I think in the first place that Chatterton was clever at Fissie
> Follogy, Pistinology, Aridology, Arography, Transmography, Phizo-
> graphy, Hogamy, Hatomy and hall that, but in the first place he eat
> very little, wickly – that is he slept very little, which he brought into a
> consumption; and what was that he took? Fissic or something – and so
> died!

Walter Scott, too, read much of Chatterton's poetry as a
young man, drawn to it not only by its medievalism but by
Chatterton's use of ancient metres, particularly his variations on
the ballad form. Scott knew the ballads 'as probably no other
poet has ever known them', writes Saintsbury, but he knew
Chatterton 'almost as well as he knew the ballads'; lines from
Chatterton's 'Unknown Knight', he suggests, may have been in
Scott's mind when he wrote *The Lay of the Last Minstrel.* In 1804

Scott wrote an important appreciation of Chatterton's work for the *Edinburgh Review*, praising his poetic achievements, colossal in relation to his youth, and deploring the unevenness of temperament, approaching insanity, which accompanied his genius. In passing, too, he attacked the host of mawkish tributes which Chatterton's fate had inspired: 'It is disgusting to hear blue stockinged ladies jingle their rhymes, and pedantic schoolmasters pipe upon their sentimental whistles a dirge over the grave of departed genius.'

Wordsworth, born in the year of Chatterton's death, immortalized him in his famous lines comparing him with Burns:

> I thought of Chatterton, the marvellous Boy,
> The sleepless Soul that perished in his pride;
> Of Him who walked in glory and in joy
> Following his plough, along the mountain-side:
> By our own spirits are we deified:
> We Poets in our youth begin in gladness;
> But there of come in the end despondency and
>   madness.

Less well known is the fact that 'Resolution and Independence', the poem in which the lines appear, is written in the metre of Chatterton's 'Ballad of Charity', and moreover on a kindred theme: in both a man is rescued from dejection or despair by the providential appearance of another – in Chatterton's poem the pilgrim is succoured by the humble priest, in Wordsworth's the poet draws comfort and spiritual sustenance from the Leech Gatherer.

Southey in oriental epics such as 'Thalaba', used exotic names and scenery in the decorative manner of Chatterton's 'African Eclogues' and like other young poets of the period (even the 'Ancient Mariner' was first printed as the 'Ancyent Marinere') tried his hand at poems in the Chattertonian medieval style.

Rossetti, who counted Chatterton's 'African Eclogues' as 'poetry absolute', saw affinities in them to 'Kubla Khan'; lines such as these from the 'Death of Nicou' may have lingered in Coleridge's subconscious as he conjured up the tumult of the 'sacred river':

On Tiber's banks, Tiber, whose waters glide
In slow meanders down to Gaigra's side;
And circling all the horrid mountains round,
Rushes impetuous to the deep profound;
Rolls o'er the ragged rocks with hideous yell;
Collects its waves beneath the earth's vast shell:
There for a while, in loud confusion hurled,
It crumbles mountains down and shakes the world.
Till borne upon the pinions of the air,
Through the rent earth the bursting waves appear;
Fiercely propelled the whitened billows rise,
Break from the cavern and ascend the skies:
Then lost and conquer'd by superior force
Through hot Arabia holds its rapid course. . . .

The words 'meander' and, a few lines later, 'mazy' in Chatterton's eclogue both appear in 'Kubla Khan':

> Five miles meandering with a mazy motion

and the Tiber, like the Alph, is sacred.

The metre of Coleridge's 'Christabel' – variations on an octo-syllabic couplet in which, while the number of accents (four) remains constant, the number of syllables may vary in correspondence 'with some transition of imagery or passion' – had an acknowledged influence on his contemporaries, above all Scott. But 'the new principle' on which it was based, as Theodore Watts-Dunton pointed out, had already been applied by Chatterton, the first poet in his century to use it. The rhythm of lines such as these:

> And Christabel saw the lady's eye,
> And nothing else saw she thereby,
> Save the boss of the shield of Sir Leoline tall,
> Which hung in a murky old niche in the wall

is captured exactly in Chatterton's 'The Unknown Knight':

> But when he threwe downe his asenglave
> Next came in Syr Botelier bold and brave,
> The dethe of manie a Saraceen,
> Theie thought him a devil from Hell's black den,

> Ne thinking that anie of mortalle menne
> Could send so manie to the grave.
> For his life to John Rumsee he render'd his thanks
> Descended from Godred the King of the Manks.

'There is no other single feature in the Rowley poems of such importance, so striking or so strange,' writes Saintsbury in his *History of English Prosody*.

But Chatterton's poetry, even to those who most admired it, could never entirely be separated from his legend. He was taken up into the Romantic cult of youth – the Romantic view of youth and childhood as the age of vision. Blake in his *Songs of Innocence*, Wordsworth in the 'Ode on the Intimations of Immortality', Coleridge as he mused by his infant's cradle in 'Frost at Midnight', saw childhood as a blessed state. Chatterton's poetic achievement, completed before the shades of adulthood had fallen, was still touched with the 'visionary gleam'. There was a sense of wonder as well as regret in the Romantic attitude towards him. Coleridge, in his poem 'On observing a blossom . . .', compares him to a flower that has bloomed too soon:

> Flower that must perish! Shall I liken thee
> To some sweet girl of too too rapid growth
> Nipped by consumption mid untimely charms?
> Or to Bristowa's bard, the wondrous boy
> An amaranth which earth scarce seemed to own
> Till disappointment came and pelting wrong
> Beat it to earth. . . .

Here, linked with the idea of youth, was the morbid element (the likeness to the consumptive girl) that was also a part of Chatterton's appeal. Death had given him charms that he would never have had in life. Cast in the role of victim he had become a symbol of the isolation and incomprehension that the poet must suffer. Hermits, solitary wanderers, the Ancient Mariner himself, were typical expressions of the poet's sense of alienation. Chatterton had personified it by his own fate. Young Romantics, feeling themselves like him in revolt, sharing his youth and creative aspirations, brooding with pleasurable melancholy on the prospect of an early grave, felt especially drawn to him. The devotion he aroused was personal. De Quincey, who writes of his dreams of Chatterton's death-bed in his diary, summed it up when he spoke of his feelings of pity, and even love, for Chatterton, 'if it be possible to feel love for one who was in his unhonoured grave before I was born'. Southey and Coleridge, perhaps because of their Bristol associations, took Chatterton especially to heart, Southey expressing his love in a practical way by his efforts on behalf of Chatterton's sister, Coleridge in one of his finest poems. To both he had been a childhood hero and his name recurs continually in the story of their early days.

Southey, as a boy in Bristol, spent hours of reverie in the church of Saint Mary Redcliffe, peopling it as Chatterton had done with figures from the medieval past, and remembering its associations with the youthful poet. 'Poor Chatterton!' he wrote, 'oft do I think upon him and sometimes indulge in the thought that had he been living he might have been my friend.'

Coleridge's 'Monody on the Death of Chatterton', his first major poem, was begun when he was still at school. Like Chatterton he wore the bluecoat uniform – Christ's Hospital was a kindred foundation to Colston's School; like Chatterton he was extraordinarily precocious, an 'inspired charity boy', whose voice would ring in philosophic discourse through the cloisters, its lofty wisdom contrasting strangely with his childish size. Coleridge was eighteen when the 'Monody' was copied into the Christ's Hospital *Commonplace Book,* where works of especial merit were recorded, but he had started it several years earlier, the first lines,

> O what a wonder seems the fear of death
> Seeing how gladly we all sink to sleep,
> Night following night for three score years and
>   ten. . . .

being written when he was only thirteen. Chatterton's early hopes before Despair, conventionally personified, has dashed them, seem to mirror Coleridge's own:

> Elate of heart and confident of Fame,
> From vales where Avon sports the Minstrel came,

> Gay as the Poet hastes along
> He meditates the future song,
> And whilst Fancy in the air
> Paints him many a vision fair
> His eyes dance rapture and his bosom glows. . . .

Coleridge returned to the 'Monody' again and again, revising and expanding it throughout his poetic career; he was still adding lines to it forty years later. Charles Lamb, Coleridge's fellow pupil at Christ's Hospital, described it as one of the finest irregular lyrics he had ever read; and it was as the author of the 'Monody' that the philanthropic Wedgwood brothers, sons of the great potter, later offered Coleridge a pension in order that he might be free to follow philosophy and poetry.

The 'Monody' first appeared in print when Coleridge was still at Cambridge, published anonymously in the introduction to a new edition of Chatterton's poems, edited by a fellow under-graduate, who acknowledged his obligation to 'an ingenious friend'. Two years later it was published under Coleridge's own name, in his first volume of poems, printed in 1796. But by this time he had met Southey and was in the first flush of enthusiasm for Pantisocracy, their Utopian scheme for founding a colony in America. He added four more verses to the poem, invoking Chatterton as a kind of honorary Pantisocrat:

> O Chatterton! that thou wert yet alive . . .

Pantisocracy was originally the brain-child of Robert Southey, christened and expanded into a system of philosophy by Coleridge, ever happy in creating vast and visionary projects, less happy in fulfilling them. Coleridge was twenty-three, Southey two years younger, a hawk-nosed undergraduate, preaching revolution and republicanism, when the two first met at Oxford. The events of the French Revolution, so shattering to their elders, were a common bond of enthusiasm between them. Southey indeed, on the death of Robespierre, had buried his face in his hands, exclaim-ing, 'I had rather have heard of the death of my own father.'

With these strong views it was unlikely that Southey should take kindly to his destined career as a clergyman, but the prospects before him were unpromising. A native of Bristol, he had fallen in love with Edith Fricker, one of a family of five sisters who, like Chatterton, lived on Redcliffe Hill, in the shadow of Saint Mary's. Miss Fricker was penniless, her mother was widowed, and she herself had been obliged to take work as a milliner.* Southey was also without resources. His father was dead, his mother badly off and he was dependent on the goodwill of a formidable aunt, who had paid for his education and brought him up, and who would certainly cut him off without a penny should he form so undistinguished an alliance. Where could he turn? The Church was out of the question, his known political views would debar him from the Civil Service. Besides, his love was for literature. He had already written a quantity of poetry and a substantial epic, *Joan of Arc*, was completed and waiting for a publisher. Love, literature and a means of subsistence must be combined. Emigration was the answer. At this point Coleridge entered his life and soon the scheme for starting a new life in America took on a dazzling aspect.

Pantisocracy was to be the system of government, an association of equals, sharing their goods in common – 'aspheterism' was Coleridge's word for this. The colony would be founded by twelve men and twelve women, of upright and liberal character. The banks of the Susquehannah River, particularly suitable 'for its excessive beauty and its freedom from hostile Indians', was to be the site. A few hours' work each day – tilling, cutting logs and so on – would supply the simple needs of the community and the rest of the time would be devoted to literature.

In the long vacation Coleridge came to visit Southey in Bristol – a Bristol as commercially prosperous as it had been in Chatterton's day, but now becoming a centre of ideas in whose atmosphere literary and political enthusiasms flourished. Here they preached Pantisocracy loud and long, collecting a group of kindred spirits round them. Southey and his Edith were now engaged, and she eager to set sail, but there was no wife – or at any rate helpmate, it not being certain whether marriage was

---

* 'Milliners of Bath' sneered Byron in *Don Juan,* when the Fricker sisters married Southey and Coleridge.

essential to Pantisocracy – for Coleridge. Conveniently, Edith had an unattached sister, Sarah. Coleridge, after backward glances at a childhood sweetheart, Mary Evans, proposed to Sarah instead and was accepted.

He was not a reliable fiancé. His engagement settled he left Bristol and after a brief stay in Cambridge, where he was still an undergraduate, went on to London where, in the back parlour of the inn where he had established himself, he whiled away his time smoking and talking with his old Christ's Hospital friend Charles Lamb. He did not communicate with Miss Fricker. Southey's remonstrances, no doubt under pressure from his future sister-in-law, were met with evasions or no reply at all. Thus procrastinating, Coleridge spent five months away from Bristol and his fellow Pantisocrats. Southey, exasperated, came up to London to fetch him and sternly took him back to Bristol.

Meanwhile Pantisocracy had suffered setbacks. Southey's aunt, on discovering the scheme, and worse still his engagement to Edith Fricker, had turned her nephew out of the house. Southey was a martyr for his beliefs. Nonetheless his suggestion soon after that Shad Weekes, his aunt's man-of-all-work, who had been invited to join the party, should not be allowed to come except in the capacity of a servant, marked a departure from the democratic ideals of Pantisocracy. Coleridge was shocked. He would have none of it. 'SHAD GOES WITH US!' he declared in emphatic capitals. 'HE IS MY BROTHER.' Southey retreated, but it was an ominous sign.

Back in Bristol Southey and Coleridge took rooms together, sharing their goods in common on the principle of aspheterism, an arrangement which soon gave Southey a grievance, since while he worked steadily on poetry and articles, Coleridge passed most of the time in talk and philosophizing. Pantisocracy was still their eventual aim, but the problem of finding sufficient funds made the date of emigration distant.

Joseph Cottle, a young Bristol bookseller with ample means and a taste for poetry, was introduced to Southey and Coleridge. Dazzled by their brilliance he determined if he could to become their publisher and patron and indulged in secret hopes that their plans would fail, lest they should be swept out of his Bristol orbit. He lent them money for their lodgings. He promised that he would publish their poems. He noted with satisfaction that Southey's enthusiasm for Pantisocracy was waning as, with his marriage still ahead and his widowed mother and sisters to support, he chafed under aspheterism with Coleridge.

Coleridge worried less about his responsibilities. The magical name of the Susquehannah still beckoned. He evoked it in his 'Monody on the Death of Chatterton':

> Yet I will love to follow the sweet dream
> Where Susquehannah pours his untamed stream;
> And on some hill, whose forest-frowning side
> Waves o'er the murmurs of his calmer tide,
> Will raise a solemn Cenotaph to thee,
> Sweet Harper of time-shrouded Minstrelsy. . . .

He was revising the poem to appear in his first volume of poetry, which Cottle was to publish. He prepared a note to accompany it in which his revolutionary sentiments were combined with indignation against Horace Walpole for his treatment of Chatterton: 'O ye who honour the name of man, rejoice that this Walpole is called a lord!' Dean Milles, the antiquarian, whose snobbish attacks on Chatterton had been such a feature of the Rowley controversy, was similarly dealt with: 'A priest; who though only a Dean, in dullness and malignity was most epis-copally eminent . . . an owl mangling a poor dead nightingale.' When Cottle, well-versed in Bristol society, remarked that a Captain Blake, whom Coleridge occasionally saw, was the son-in-law of this same Dean, Coleridge recoiled in mock horror. 'What,' he said, 'the man with the great sword?' 'The same,' said Cottle. 'Then,' said Coleridge with assumed gravity, 'I will suppress this note on Chatterton; the fellow will have my head off before I am aware.'

The note was indeed suppressed, but not, presumably, for fear of Captain Blake's sword, though the sight of it, said Coleridge, 'was enough to send half a dozen poets scampering up Parnassus, as though hunted by a wild mastodon'.

Like a bolt from the blue, Southey announced his abandonment of Pantisocracy. A rich uncle had offered him financial security if he would promise to take up the study of law: and as a further inducement had offered him a six months' tour of Portugal before he started. It was enough to disentangle him finally. He married Edith Fricker secretly – his uncle, like his aunt, would not have approved – handed her to the care of Joseph Cottle and his sisters as a parlour boarder and set off for Lisbon. The episode, as far as he was concerned, was over.

Coleridge was stunned. It was a black betrayal. Now his only link with Pantisocracy was the bride he had chosen to accompany him to America. Cottle generously offered him a guinea and a half for every hundred lines of poetry he produced, and with this and an advance of thirty guineas on his poems he felt secure enough to marry. The wedding took place in Saint Mary Redcliffe – 'Poor Chatterton's church,' said Coleridge with gloomy relish. Perhaps the setting really was ill-omened, for the marriage, though it started happily enough, turned out to be a disaster. The pair were totally unsuited. Southey was to pay a heavy price for urging on the marriage in the years in the Lake District when, Coleridge having deserted his family, he found himself responsible for his sister-in-law and her children, while Coleridge, enthralled by opium, disappeared to London.

Joseph Cottle remained friends with both the poets, though the abandonment of Pantisocracy left a breach between the brothers-in-law which was never entirely healed. A few years later Southey had returned to Bristol and was seeing as much as ever of his publisher. He had always retained his fervent interest in his fellow Bristolian Chatterton. Now it came to his notice that Chatterton's sister, Mrs Newton, was in grave financial difficulties, recently widowed and with a child to support. Her brother's fame, so profitable to Catcott and Croft, had brought little benefit to his relations. Their mother had died of cancer a few years previously, saved from total indigence by the kindness of the poetess Hannah More. ('You should have married Chatterton,' Doctor Johnson teased her, 'that posterity might have seen a propagation of poets.')

Southey and Cottle, as a task of pure charity, determined to bring out a new edition of Chatterton's poems – which had hitherto served only 'to fatten booksellers' – and to present the proceeds to his sister.

A subscription list was opened, and the public's support was sought for in the columns of the *Monthly Magazine*. Southey, rightly concluding that support might not be overwhelming without some revival of controversy, found a convenient villain to add spice to the tale of Mrs Newton's plight. The villain was Sir Herbert Croft, whose shady behaviour in 'borrowing' Chatterton's letters from his family made a good excuse for righteous indignation. Nearly twenty years had passed since the publication of *Love and Madness*, – 'It has passed into the language,' said Sir Herbert – so righteous indignation might seem somewhat overdue. But there was no doubt that he had not behaved well. He had published Chatterton's letters without the knowledge or consent of his family; and though he had made a great deal of money from *Love and Madness*, which ran into seven editions, it was only after indignant requests from Mrs Chatterton that he had offered any payment at all – a grudging £10 to be shared between mother and daughter. On Mrs Chatterton's death her daughter had written once again, demanding further reparation and threatening to make his conduct public; Chatterton's family, replied Sir Herbert insultingly, had no further claim on him, however, if given suitable assurances as to their *moral* character by the local clergyman, he would consider the matter.

Sir Herbert's villainies having been set out in the *Monthly Magazine* of November 1799, the angry baronet took the next three issues of the rival *Gentleman's Magazine* to reply. 'I have ever reverenced the little finger of Chatterton more than Mr Southey knows how to respect the poor boy's whole body,' he announced indignantly, but his explanations were unconvincing and on the principle that attack is the best defence he devoted the larger part of his reply to sneers at Southey, 'who writes bad poetry like bad prose', and to ridiculing Pantisocracy. He could not deny, however, having published the letters for his personal profit and without the consent of Chatterton's family; these two points, as Southey pointed out, were enough to condemn him, and Sir Herbert, discredited, was seen to lose the argument.

Despite this exchange a sufficient number of subscribers was slow in coming and the book hung fire for two years until, in 1802, the publishers Longman and Rees agreed to take it on. Southey set to work on the editing and transcribing of Chatterton's poems, a labour of love which he found more demanding than he had expected, with Rowley's archaisms a constant stumbling-block. Cottle was called in to provide notes and an appendix on the Rowley controversy. Southey laughed privately at the 'Cottleisms' in the text – Cottle was no stylist – but needed no convincing as to the authorship of the poems.

'The Rowley question has long been dismissed from my thoughts,' he wrote to a friend.

In fact since I had the smallest acquaintance with old English litera-
ture I was perfectly convinced that it was utterly impossible the poems could be genuine. I will however mention one decisive argument, which I owe to a friend. The little facsimile of Canynge's feast [see back cover], contains manifest proofs that the hand writing is feigned, for if you will examine it you will find that the letter 'e' is written in some eighteen or twenty different ways. . . .

('Oh!' quipped Charles Lamb when this proof was shown to him, 'that must have been written by one of the "mob of gentlemen who write with ease". ')

An examination of Barrett's long-hoarded parchment 'origin-als' had provided further confirmation. Barrett having left them on his death to the pro-Rowley Dr Glynn, Glynn had bequeathed them in 1800 to the British Museum, where Southey and Cottle had been allowed to examine them. Their spuriousness was immediately evident. It was hardly to be wondered at, said Southey, that the advocates of Rowley should have deduced so few of their arguments from the manuscripts.

Mrs Newton, whose attitude throughout the Rowley debate had been non-committal, showed no surprise when Cottle informed her that the poems were her brother's; her face lit up, he reported, and with a singularly arch smile she replied, 'Aye to

REV.ᴰ Jˢ. HACKMAN.

MISS REAY.

Neele & Stockley fc. 352 Strand.

Memorial engraving of James Hackman and Martha Reay, 1780. Hackman wears a circle of black plaster to cover the wound of his suicide attempt. The murder of Miss Reay at Covent Garden is shown beneath.

The Chatterton of
the French
Romantics. *Above,*
Fourau's painting
of 1842 shows
Chatterton
contemplating the
phial of poison,
while Kitty Bell
peeps round the
doorway. *Below,*
the frontispiece of
Vigny's *Chatterton*
of 1835. The
author's portrait is
upheld by angels;
Kitty Bell and
Chatterton stand at
the foot of the fatal
staircase.

CHATTERTON

PUBLIE
PAR
HIPPOLYTE
SOUVERAIN
1835

be sure; anybody could have seen that with half an eye.'

Doctor Gregory's life of Chatterton for the *Biographia Britannica* (ironically a commission at first given to Croft) was reprinted in the introduction to the book. 'It is a bad work,' said Southey. 'Coleridge should write a new one, or if he declines it, let it devolve on me.' 'I will certainly write a preliminary essay,' said Coleridge, but like so many other projected works of his it did not get written, nor could Southey find the time. Coleridge's 'Monody', however, did appear in the introduction, though at first he had been reluctant to have it used, finding its images overblown: 'On a life so full of heartgoing *realities* as poor Chatterton's to find such shadowy nobodies as cherub winged *Death*, trees of *Hope*, bare bosomed *Affection* and simpering *Peace*, makes one's blood circulate like ipecacuhana,' he wrote to Southey. However, he let himself be persuaded, and the poem appeared, the lines on the Susquehanna perhaps a subtle reproach to his brother-in-law.

The book, with Wordsworth's name among the subscribers, appeared in 1803. 'Well done, good and faithful editor,' wrote Southey to Cottle. The profits brought in nearly £400 for Chatterton's sister, so the fortune as well as the fame he had sought for his family seemed made at last. Southey, his good deed done, heaved a sigh of relief and returned to his work on a monumental history of Portugal. Now that the poems were published and the money collected, there was, he felt, in writing to a friend, no impropriety in mentioning what could not be said before –

that there was a taint of insanity in the family. His sister was once confined and this is the key to the eccentricities of his life and the deplorable rashness of his death. Of the honour which he has gained in his own country [he went on], there is one whimsical instance. Ten years ago a leathern breeches maker and undertaker had upon his shop card an urn 'Sacred to the memory of Chatterton'. One of these cards is *penes me* as the expression is, and perhaps Mr Haslewood [a contemporary collector of Chattertonania] in his extraordinary collection upon the subject has nothing more curious.

H

11 The Poet's Poet: Keats

O Chatterton! How very sad thy fate!
Dear child of sorrow – son of misery!
How soon the film of death obscur'd that eye,
Whence Genius mildly flash'd, and high debate.
How soon that voice, majestic and elate,
Melted in dying numbers! Oh! how nigh
Was night to thy fair morning. Thou didst die
A half blown flow'ret which cold blasts amate.
But this is past: thou art among the stars
Of highest Heaven: to the rolling spheres
Thou sweetest singest: nought thy hymning mars
Above the ingrate world and human fears.
On earth the good man base detraction bars
From thy fair name, and waters it with tears.

JOHN KEATS (1815)

Byron, Shelley and Keats, by dying young, seemed to confirm the Romantic association between genius and early death; in death at least Chatterton could be seen as their precursor. In life their attitudes to him varied widely, Byron near-indifferent, Keats whole hearted in his devotion.

Byron, reacting perhaps against the enthusiasm of the 'pond poets' for Chatterton, had little good to say of him. 'Chatterton, I think, was mad,' he wrote of his death, and elsewhere, while criticizing the vulgarity of contemporary poets, exempted Chatterton, along with Burns and Wordsworth: 'Chatterton is never vulgar.'

Shelley was more enthusiastic. Among his juvenilia are imitations of Chatterton's antique style and his early poem 'Ghasta or the Avenging Demon' starts with a direct plagiarism of Chatterton's 'Minstrels' Roundelay'.

Hark! the ravenne flappes hys wynge
In the briered dell below;

> Hark! the dethe-owle loud doth synge
> To the nyghte-mares as heie goe,

writes Chatterton. These are Shelley's lines:

> Hark! the owlet flaps her wing
> In the pathless dell beneath;
> Hark! night ravens loudly sing
> Tidings of despair and death.

Shelley soon abandoned his interest, though he returns to Chatterton in 'Adonais'. But Keats's love for Chatterton, given expression in one of his earliest sonnets, developed and continued throughout his poetic life. 'Everybody now knows what was then known to his friends,' wrote Benjamin Bailey in his recollections of Keats, 'that Keats was an ardent admirer of Chatterton. The melody of the verses of "the 'marvellous boy who perished in his pride" enchanted the author of "Endymion"....'

In letters, poetry and conversation Keats returned to Chatterton time and again. He loved to recite his poetry, declaiming the 'Ballad of Charles Bawdin', recalled one listener, 'with an enthusiasm such as only a true poet could feel'. He dedicated 'Endymion', his first major poem, to Chatterton's memory; and in his last months of writing, before his decline into consumption, he returned to Chatterton once more as 'the purest writer in the English language'. He ever spoke of him, said Lord Houghton, Keats's first biographer, with a kind of prescient sympathy.

Keats was not a 'marvellous boy' in the sense that Chatterton had been, and the poems of his teens show no special precocity. The sonnet to Chatterton – almost his first attempt in that form – was written when he was eighteen:

> O Chatterton! How very sad thy fate!....

Conventionally romantic, it owes something to Coleridge's 'Monody', which Keats would have read in the preface to the Southey Cottle edition of Chatterton's poems, and borrows from Chatterton, who had borrowed it from Spenser, the archaism 'amate' – 'a half blown flow'ret which cold blasts amate'. To Chatterton, as to Keats, who ran through Spenser's poetry 'like

a horse in a spring meadow', Spenser was an important source
of inspiration.

Eighteen months later Chatterton appears again in the 'Epistle
to George Felton Matthew' – a poetical friend of Keats, 'languid
and melancholy . . . thoughtful beyond my years' as he described
himself in a memoir of their friendship. Faintly ridiculous though
he sounds, he was Keats's first friend with ambitions as a poet,
and in his first enthusiasm – which he soon outgrew – Keats
envisaged a poetic brotherhood with him, in which they would
flee the cares of the world (and by implication Keats's medical
studies) together, for some secluded and romantic grove:

> Where we may soft humanity put on
> And sit and rhyme and think of Chatterton . . .
> And mourn the fearful dearth of human kindness
> To those who strive with the bright golden wing
> Of genius, to flap away each sting
> Thrown by the pitiless world. . . .

Poetry here is still an Arcadian retreat from reality and Chatterton
a romantic symbol. But in the poem which is regarded as the
preface to Keats's mature work, and in which his sense of vocation
was crystallized, Chatterton is considered more seriously as Keats
reflects on the poetry of his native land and the poets, past and
present, who must guide him. He denounces the sterile
influence of Pope on the poetry of the eighteenth century – a
denunciation which roused Byron to a frenzy of irritation when
the poem appeared – remembering Chatterton as a herald in the
empty age, one of those

> . . . lone spirits who could proudly sing
> Their youth away and die. . . .

The poem was 'Sleep and Poetry'. Its first draft was composed
in the house of Leigh Hunt, the poet and editor of the liberal
paper the *Examiner*, whom Keats had met a few months before,
in the summer of 1816. The meeting had been a turning-point for
Keats, long an admirer of Hunt, both as a poet and for the
courageous radicalism which had landed him in prison three
years before for libelling the Prince Regent. Hunt, in his turn,

immediately recognizing Keats's exceptional gifts – as he was to those of Shelley that same year – had swept him into the literary and artistic circle over which he presided in his untidy, pretty, book-filled cottage. In his company and that of his friends, Keats had found for the first time the stimulation of professional writers and poets. Now, in the library of Hunt's house, where, after a late evening, a makeshift bed had been made up on the sofa, surrounded by busts and scenes from classical mythology (a setting evoked in the last lines of the poem), Keats gathered up his thoughts on the meaning of poetry, seeing it as something to be found not only in Arcadia, but in the strife and anguish of the human heart; and, perhaps with premonition, made his famous plea – it was not much to ask at twenty-one – for ten more years of life.

> O for ten years, that I may overwhelm
> Myself in poetry; so I may do the deed
> That my own soul has to myself decreed . . .

'Sleep and Poetry' was the poetic expression of Keats's determination to devote his life to poetry. In practical terms it meant the abandonment of his all but completed medical training and the decision to live by his pen. Thanks to Leigh Hunt he had found a publisher for a volume of his early poems, of which 'Sleep and Poetry' was the last, and these, with a dedicatory sonnet to Hunt, appeared in the spring of 1817. They attracted little critical notice.

But Keats, not discouraged, had already set his sights on a far more ambitious goal – the writing of 'Endymion', an epic poem on a huge Miltonic scale. In April, leaving London for the Isle of Wight, he began work in solitude, away from the influence of friends. The first line of the poem was already penned – 'A thing of beauty is a joy for ever'; the rest of his task, he felt, towered like a cliff above him.

The story of Endymion, as Keats wrote in one of his delightful, faintly avuncular letters to his fourteen-year-old sister Fanny, was that of 'a young handsome shepherd who fed his flock on a Mountain's side called Latmus little thinking that such a beautiful creature as the Moon had fallen mad in love with him; however so it was; and when he was asleep on the grass she used to come down from heaven and admire him excessively. . . .' Endymion's search for the elusive goddess of the moon leads him through an enchanted landscape; the poem is a fairy tale, 'a kind of magic toy', as Rossetti described it. But at a deeper level it can be seen as an allegory of the poet's search for beauty, a beauty symbolized by the moon. The poem evades too close an interpretation – Keats himself, weary of it towards the end and later discouraged by hostile criticism, gave no key to its meaning; but in one episode, the legend of Glaucus and Scylla, Chatterton, it is possible, may play a symbolic part.

The episode runs thus. In the third book of the poem Endymion, as he wanders across the floor of the sea, comes upon Glaucus, an aged, palsied man, sitting on a rock. Glaucus tells him of his enchantment by Circe, and of the death of his true love, Scylla. He can be restored to his youthful form, and Scylla to life, only through the agency of Endymion, whose coming has been foretold in a scroll – a scroll he had snatched from a drowning old man's hand as the waves of a shipwreck engulfed him. Since then, for a thousand years it has been the task of Glaucus to enshrine the bodies of all lovers who have been drowned at sea, together with that of Scylla, in a crystal edifice beneath the water. Now, stuttering with joy at the prospect of deliverance, he leads Endymion to this shrine and tearing his scroll in tiny pieces bids Endymion strew the 'mincèd leaves' of parchment on him, and on the rows of dead. As the fragments are scattered Glaucus is transformed into a radiant youth; Scylla is restored; the drowned lovers spring to life.

'It may be prying too curiously to seek to establish the exact meaning of the Keatsian myth,' says Chatterton's biographer Meyerstein; but Endymion's liberation of Glaucus and the enshrined dead, he suggests, may be taken for the freeing of poetry from the death-like bondage of eighteenth-century convention, the scattered fragments of parchment for those scraps of manuscript found at Chatterton's death – a circumstance familiar to anyone who had read his life – the reviving magic the new spirit which Chatterton had brought to English poetry.

Whatever Chatterton's significance here, it was to his memory

that Keats dedicated 'Endymion', his first version of the dedication
running thus:

> Inscribed
> with every feeling of pride and regret
> and with a 'bowed mind'
> to the memory of the most English of poets except
>   Shakespeare,
> Thomas Chatterton

The preface which accompanied the dedication concluded somewhat defiantly:

One word more – for we cannot help but see our own affairs in
every point of view – should anyone call my dedication to Chatterton
affected I answer as followeth: 'Were I dead, sir, I should like a book
dedicated to me.'

But this version, on the advice of his friend Reynolds, was abandoned for a second preface and the final dedication read simply,

Inscribed to the memory of Thomas Chatterton.

'Endymion' had taken eight months to write, a quarter of
Keats's serious writing life, and comprised almost half of all the
poetry published in his lifetime. That it was uneven and full of
faults he knew, but in it he had been working out his own philosophy: 'In Endymion, I leaped headlong into the sea, and thereby
have become better acquainted with the Soundings, the quicksands
and the rocks, than if I had stayed on the green shore and piped a
silly pipe and took tea and comfortable advice.'

In this stalwart spirit Keats faced the storm of criticism and
derision which greeted the publication of 'Endymion', his
denunciation in *Blackwood's Magazine* under the heading of 'The
Cockney School of Poetry': 'Back to the shop Master John, back
to the plasters, pills and ointment boxes . . .'

Even Leigh Hunt failed to support him, delaying his review
for several months, and then devoting it to his own theories on
poetry. But to one friend, Richard Woodhouse, lawyer and legal
adviser to Keats's publishers, 'Endymion' was a work of genius,
which he declared, if it were to be compared to Shakespeare's

'Venus and Adonis', written at about the same age, would be found to contain more beauties and more promise of excellence. Unknown to Keats, Woodhouse had already done much to smooth his way with his publishers, often annoyed by Keats's *rodomontade* and excitability, and later, again unknown to Keats, had advanced them £50 from his own small income to advance to him because, as he wrote, 'What people regret they could not do for Shakespeare or Chatterton, because he did not live in their time, that (with due regard to certain expediencies) I would embody into a rational principle and do for Keats.'

Now, in writing to Keats on the reception of 'Endymion', he recalled Chatterton's hostile reception by the world as he exhorted Keats to ignore the crassness and malice of the reviewers – an exhortation repeated shortly after in a letter which he enclosed for Keats from Jane Porter, a lady novelist.

I hope [wrote Miss Porter], the ill natured review will not have damped such true Parnassian fire - it ought not for when life is granted to the possessor it always burns its brilliant way through every obstacle. Had Chatterton possessed sufficient manliness of mind to show the magnanimity of Patience, and been aware that great talents have a commission from Heaven, he would not have deserted his post and his name might have posed with Milton.

To this enthusiastic lady Woodhouse offered Keats an introduction, but Keats, though amused enough to recount the offer to his brother, turned it down.

Chatterton's potential was not always rated so high. Earlier that year he was briskly dismissed by Hazlitt, in his series of lectures on the English poets, at which Keats, who ranked Hazlitt's literary criticism as one of 'the three things to rejoice at in this Age', was a regular attender. Hazlitt, pale as death and shaking with nerves at his first lecture, had got into his stride as the series went on. His audiences were packed to the ceiling, and his uncompromising opinions attracted boos and hisses – to which he paid not the slightest attention – in equal measure with applause. He turned to Chatterton at the conclusion of the sixth of his lectures, and having quoted Wordsworth's famous lines, linking his name with Burns, continued drily:

I am loth to put assunder what so great an authority has joined together; but I cannot find in Chatterton's works anything so extraordinary as the age at which they were written. . . . He did not show extraordinary powers of genius but extraordinary precocity. Nor do I believe he would have written better had he lived. He knew this himself or he would have lived. Great geniuses like great kings have too much to think of to kill themselves. . . .

On Keats, whose young brother Tom was sinking into his final illness, and already haunted by the fear that he too might die before his work was completed, these words must have struck a chill. 'I hear Hazlitt's lectures regularly,' he wrote to his brothers, '. . . I was very disappointed by his treatment of Chatterton.' He must have made his feeling known, because Hazlitt, who had met Keats often, with Leigh Hunt and others, began his next lecture by expressing his regret that what he had said about Chatterton 'should have given dissatisfaction to some persons with whom I would willingly agree on all such matters'. Defending his opinion he quoted some of the eulogistic nonsense heaped by Sir Herbert Croft and others on Chatterton's memory, and took as his touchstone the fact that Chatterton's poems, as opposed to his pathetic fate, did not spring readily to the mind, and that he had never heard anyone speak of any of his works as if it were an old, well-known favourite – a dictum to which Keats provided a notable exception. Then, to make amends, he quoted in full the 'Minstrels' Roundelay' in *Ælla*, which he considered Chatterton's best work, and which, as he must have known, was an especial favourite of Keats.

In the autumn of 1819, when Keats's last poems were written, Chatterton was much in his mind as he turned away from the elaborate Miltonic style which had influenced him in his 'Hyperion' to a simpler and more natural manner:

The purest English I think – or what ought to be the purest – is Chatterton's. The language had existed long enough to be entirely uncorrupted of Chaucer's gallicisms and still the old words are used – Chatterton's language is entirely northern – I prefer the native music of it to Milton's cut by feet. I have but lately stood on my guard against Milton.

'I somehow always associate Chatterton with Autumn,' he wrote in another letter that day. It was September. The weather was glorious:

How beautiful the season is now, how fine the air. A temperate sharpness about it. Really without joking chaste weather. Dian skies – I never liked stubble fields so much as now – Aye better than the chilly green of the spring. Somehow a stubble plain looks warm – in the same way that some pictures look warm. This struck me so much in my Sunday's walk that I composed upon it.

The poem was the 'Ode to Autumn', the last of Keats's great odes. In its simplicity and purity, as well as in its images, it recalls the third 'Minstrel's Song' from Chatterton's *Ælla* which Keats had been rereading:

> Whanne Autumne blake and sonne-brente doe
>   appere,
> With hys goulde honde guylteynge the falleynge lefe,
> Bryngeynge oppe Wynterr to folfylle the yere,
> Beerynge uponne hys backe the riped shefe;
> Whan al the hyls wythe woddie sede ys whyte;
> Whanne levynne fyres and lemes do mete from far
>   the syghte;
>
> Whann the fayre apple, rudde as even skie,
> Do bende the trees unto the fructyle grounde;
> When joicie peres and berries of blacke die,
> Do daunce yn ayre and call the eyne around;
> Thann, bee the even foule, or even fayre,
> Meethynckes mie hartys joie ys steynced wyth
>   somme care.

The idea of autumn as a reaper is central to Keats's ode and comes from Chatterton; from Chatterton too comes the image of apples bending down the trees:

> To bend with apples the mossed cottag'd trees,

while in the first draft of the poem there is a direct borrowing from Chatterton in the line:

> While a *gold* cloud *gilds* the soft dying day,

changed in the final version to:

> While barred clouds bloom the soft dying day.

Keats's reading of *Ælla*, too, is reflected in his 'Eve of Saint Mark', which he had started earlier that year, and taken up again that autumn, perhaps inspired by the peaceful surroundings of Winchester, where he had taken lodgings. 'I think it will give you the sensation of walking about an old County town in a coolish evening,' he wrote, on transcribing it in a letter to his brother. It is a Gothic tale, written in the metre of Chatterton; the name of the heroine, Bertha, is that of the heroine in *Ælla*,

> Bertha was a maiden fair
> Dwelling in th' old Minster square. . . .

All day long she sits reading in her room from an ancient volume, rich with golden illuminations; as dusk falls she still pores over its pages in which, in ancient English no more authentic than Chatterton's, is recounted the legend of Saint Mark – on the eve of Saint Mark, so the legend runs, the ghosts of all those who are to die in the next year will appear.

The new poem was never finished. Did the legend run too close to life? By December increasing illness had almost put a stop to Keats's work. On 3 February he suffered the first haemorrhage of the lungs, the haemorrhage in which he read his death warrant. His 'posthumous life' thereafter stretched on for one agonizing year till his death in Rome in 1820, at the age of just twenty-five. In 'Adonais', Shelley's beautiful elegy on Keats's death, Chatterton's name was associated with his for the last time, as Shelley placed him by his side, among

> The inheritors of unfulfilled renown . . .
> Chatterton rose pale; his solemn agony
> Had not yet faded from him . . .

12 Alfred de Vigny and 'Chatterton'

The trouble began with Chatterton. Since that little fool saw fit to poison himself to the frantic applause of a still more foolish audience, certain young men have been mad enough to follow his example. They think that suicide is still the best way to prove one's genius. It's an odd piece of logic but the custom seems common today.

PARISIAN DIARIST: 1836

The Romantic Movement in France was at its height when Alfred de Vigny's *Chatterton* opened at the Théâtre Français in 1835. Paris was alight with the enthusiasm of a generation which, brought up amid the fanfares of the Napoleonic Wars, and now deprived of its stirring ideals, had turned its ardour to the arts instead, flinging themselves into revolt against the restraints of academic art and literature. Their fiercest battles were fought in the theatre, where the measured alexandrines and classical unities which had held sway for two centuries were swept aside in favour of rousing historical dramas. Toledo steel flashed at hip and thigh, Walter Scott and Shakespeare were admired and acknowledged influences. The famous first night of Victor Hugo's *Hernani* in 1830, with its deliberate defiance of the classic traditions, was the all-out attack of the Romantic Movement, the outrage of the traditionalists reaching its climax when, to the wild applause of the young Romantics, the alexandrine, sacred and immutable verse form, was broken in mid-phrase.

Chatterton, hailed with equal enthusiasm five years later, was pitched in a totally different key. Nothing could be greater than the contrast between its simplicity and the inflated melodrama of *Hernani*. It was written in prose, not verse, in language that was deliberately flat, emotion conveyed by silence or an everyday phrase. The mood foreshadowed modern theatre, the action was negligible, the problem a psychological one. Balzac summarized it coarsely: 'First Act: shall I kill myself? Second Act: I should kill myself. Third Act: I do kill myself.' But its theme, the perpetual martyrdom of the poet in an uncomprehending society, was passionately Romantic and it touched a ready chord in the hearts of those who watched. When the final curtain fell there was a moment of stunned silence, then the whole house rose to its feet with applause that lasted for twenty minutes. Vigny's friends flung their arms round his neck weeping; he himself was in tears.

Queen Marie Amélie was watching from the royal box and the expensive seats were filled by fashionable Parisians, but the parterre was crowded with Chatterton's spiritual comrades – pale young men, wrote their comrade Théophile Gautier, whose burning eyes proclaimed their belief that Art and Poetry were the only possible occupations on earth, while their flowing hair and extraordinary clothes demonstrated their scorn for the rest of the audience, conventionally dressed for a first night. Chatterton was their poet, a martyr in their cause.

The play launched a craze for suicide '*à la Chatterton*'. The cult that had started with Werther had reached its apogee. 'It was a mania confirmed with vows by all the Renés, all the Chattertons, that one must become a great poet and die,' said Sainte-Beuve.

Never had a generation seemed so in love with the idea of death. Poets swooned over corpses, drank wine from skulls, slept in coffins. The young Alfred de Musset, admiring a beautiful view, gave it the highest praise at his command: 'Ah, what a wonderful place to kill oneself.'

The Government, alarmed by the morbid tendencies of literary youth, held a debate to discuss the deplorable influence of *Chatterton*. The Minister of the Interior complained of being plagued by letters from starving geniuses, threatening to kill themselves unless the State came to their aid; and a Count Maillé de Latour-Landry, moved by Vigny's picture of the poet's plight, founded a prize for struggling poets, to be administered by the Académie Française.

Vigny himself was appalled by the play's effect. He had meant to plead the cause of young writers, not to encourage them to kill themselves. He found himself cast into the role of protector of potential Chattertons. He played it nobly, encouraging, and though far from rich, financing those he considered deserving. He could be importunate on a protégé's behalf – but was always too proud to ask a favour for himself. '*Il se faisait le pontife des jeunes esprits malheureux,*'* commented Sainte-Beuve waspishly. He admired Vigny but thought he took himself too seriously.

Everything about Vigny conveyed the impression of nobility and moral beauty. Sainte-Beuve, malicious as always, had nicknamed him the Seraph, and indeed he had the looks of an angel – delicate features, deep-set grey eyes, golden hair curling round a lofty brow. He was an aristocrat whose parents had seen brothers and cousins die on the guillotine. From them he had imbibed a sense of caste and a sombre outlook which combined with his natural timidity to make him seem cold and withdrawn. He seemed totally dissimilar to his comrades-in-arms, who with him dominated the new movement in the theatre – Victor Hugo and Alexandre Dumas, both of them coarse of feature and brimming over with panache and vitality. Nor, superficially at least, could he have chosen a greater opposite than his mistress, the actress Marie Dorval, for whom he created her greatest role as the heroine of *Chatterton*.

Marie Dorval was the darling of Romantic theatre-goers. She was unashamedly of the people, intuitive, witty and natural to the point of abandon. She had a hoarse, breathless voice which could switch from tremulous emotion to wild laughter or a fishwife tirade in a moment. Her large melancholy eyes could convey unbearable pathos or sparkle with gaiety. She was frail, dark, poetic – 'better than pretty she was charming,' wrote George Sand, 'and yet she was pretty but so charming that it was unnecessary.'

The daughter of strolling players, with a miserable childhood and youth behind her, she had made her name at the popular Porte-Saint-Martin Theatre, home of vaudeville and improbable melodrama. Dumas and Victor Hugo as well as Vigny vied to

* 'He made himself the pontiff of unhappy youth.'

write plays for her, and her position in the theatre was further strengthened by her marriage to the director Toussaint Merle. Merle, whom 'autumn detached from Venus', was a complaisant husband, as he had need to be. Dorval's affairs were notorious.

Vigny met her in 1829. She was sitting in a café with Alexandre Dumas when he came in. Dumas introduced them, and left them at the same table while he got up to greet other acquaintances.

Some months later Dumas called to see Dorval with the script of a new play under his arm. Her husband was away and he was surprised at the formality of her greeting.

'Is that how you kiss your old friends?'
'I'm becoming like Marion Delorme; I've taken up virginity again.'
'Impossible!'
'Word of honour. I'm becoming *sage*.'
'And who the devil has brought this about?'
'Alfred de Vigny.'
'You love him?'
'I'm crazy about him . . . he writes poetry for me.'
'In that case my dear, let me congratulate you; in the first place Vigny is a poet of immense talent; and secondly he is a real gentleman . . .'
'He calls me his angel.'
'Bravo!'
'The other day I had a little spot on my shoulder, he said it was my wings which were growing . . .'

But the Seraph had met with a fallen angel. The quicksilver shifts of emotion which made Marie Dorval a great actress did not make for stability, and the insecurity of her youth had left an indelible mark. She was too volatile for constancy. Vigny, whose ideas of passion were exalted, suffered tortures of jealousy over her incidental infidelities and, worse still, suspected her of nameless sins with George Sand, whose waistcoat, trousers and cigars gave rise to grave doubts.

The affair dragged on for seven years, years of increasing unhappiness for both. The year 1837 saw the entry in Vigny's diary, RUPTURE, marked with two crossed swords. He never wrote another play, and from the ivory tower of his country estate, he anathematized the treachery of women in his poem 'La

Colère de Samson'. Marie Dorval, her equilibrium destroyed, spiralled down into debt and theatrical oblivion, her last years spent dragging the rags of her former glories round the provincial theatres of France as miserably as her first.

Chatterton had been the highspot of her career. It was Vigny's last play for her, written in seventeen nights of concentrated inspiration, his feelings so intense, he told a friend, that at times he fainted from emotion. It was the last play he ever wrote. The wounds he had received at her hands, his sense of loneliness and spiritual isolation, were projected onto the pale and ardent figure of Chatterton, while in his gentle trembling heroine Marie Dorval was transformed into the ideal woman he had failed to find in life.

There was no trace of a heroine in Chatterton's life, as Vigny was well aware. Chatterton had already aroused considerable interest in France. The Lake Poets and their enthusiasm for 'the marvellous boy' were known to the young Romantics, and in 1825 the poet Henri Latouche had composed a three-hundred-line elegy lamenting Chatterton's fate. This, though it was not published until 1833, Vigny read privately; thereafter he had studied Chatterton's life and poetry in some detail, and at the literary *salon* of Charles Nodier, once secretary to Sir Herbert Croft, must have come across *Love and Madness*. But in the play this did not matter: 'Le poète était tout . . . un exemple à jamais déplorable d'un noble misère.'* Chatterton's martyrdom was symbolic of the fate of all genius, consistently rejected and mis-understood by society. The facts could be readjusted round the theme. Hence the introduction of a heroine, Kitty Bell, whose love for Chatterton and whose sensitive response to his genius inevitably link her with his tragedy.

Kitty Bell had first appeared in Vigny's biographical novel *Stello*, in which Chatterton is one of three heroes, each the victim of a different form of society – the poet Gilbert, starved under the *ancien régime*, Chatterton driven to his death under a constitutional monarchy, André Chenier guillotined during the French Revolution. Whatever the regime, the possessor of genius will always be an outcast. The argument is given in the form of a dialogue

* 'The poet was everything . . . a forever pitiable example of noble misery.'

The operatic Chatterton: Thomas Salignac, the tenor who took the title part in Leoncavallo's opera in Nice, 1905.

Francis Thompson in 1888, whose vision of Chatterton averted an attempt at suicide.

E. H. W. Meyerstein, the poet, and Chatterton's biographer. This portrait of him was painted by Philip Connard in 1928.

between Stello, a beautiful young man steeped in Romantic dissatisfaction, and the Docteur Noir, an enigmatic figure who prescribes for his melancholy, like a nineteenth-century Shaharazade. The doctor's 'Consultations' or stories last through a stifling summer night while Stello tosses feverishly on his couch.

The central episode concerns Chatterton. Kitty Bell first appears on a foggy day in her little shop, close to the Houses of Parliament, where she sells sweetmeats, *'les mince pies'*, to the young bucks of the town, rebuffing their chaff with modest dignity. She is typically English, fair-haired, tall, with long hands and feet, slightly gauche. Her husband, Chatterton's landlord, is coarse and overbearing; her whole devotion is fixed on her two children and, though she dares not admit it to herself, on the seventeen-year-old boy in their garret room.

Chatterton faces despair. He has failed to sell his poems and must now pay his debts by selling his own body for medical research. His last hope is for help from the Mayor, Lord Beckford, a friend of his late father. Beckford sweeps in radiating gross good humour and humming 'Rule Britannia'. Paying no attention to Chatterton's proffered sheaf of poems, he offers him the post of valet in his household. Crushed by this last humiliation, Chatterton flings his manuscripts into the fire and drinks the fatal draught. As he dies he gasps out his love for Kitty Bell; she dies soon after of a broken heart.

These are the bones of the play, and its plot is the same in essentials. But in the play, all is distilled, the faintly ludicrous touches of local colour have disappeared, the minor characters, the insensitive Beckford, a pair of frivolous *milords*, all express the different attitudes of Philistines in the face of genius. Most significant of all, the landlord, John Bell, is given a new dimension: he is shown as a capitalist and industrialist, an exploiter of his workers; the worker, like the poet, is crushed by an oppressive society, which refuses him a fair reward for his labour.

Marie Dorval, whose theatrical instinct was so sure that even Dumas took corrections from her, immediately grasped the possibilities of the play, despite its unfashionable simplicity. But the first reading was turned down unanimously by the Théâtre

I

Français, the holy of holies of the French theatre, and it was only through the intervention of the Queen and the Duke of Orléans (who supported Vigny as a nobleman and former officer) that the decision was reversed. The Théâtre Français were forced to give way, but they set their faces against the casting of Marie Dorval as Kitty Bell. Despite her fame they had consistently refused to accept 'an actress of the boulevards'. Her reputation, plebeian accent and her naturalism were anathema to the older actresses of the Théâtre Français, trained in the stylized manner of the classical school, and their intrigues against her had hitherto succeeded in keeping her out. But Vigny, whose love for Dorval had always been reflected in his concern for her career, was determined that her talents should receive recognition. He fought the matter through against intense opposition. Marie Dorval obtained the part.

The other actors were icily antagonistic during the rehearsals. The set centred round a spiral staircase which led up to Chatterton's room. From the top of this, she announced, she would stage her dying fall. She refused to rehearse her *dégringolade*, and the company, disapproving and curious, had to wait for the first night to see the acrobatic and audacious climax.

The first night was her triumph, the vindication of *Chatterton* and Dorval. She played opposite Geoffroy: bitter, sarcastic, dry in his manner, he was one of the great actors of the Romantic age. 'To this day,' wrote Maxime du Camp, who was carried out fainting at the end of the play, 'when Chatterton is mentioned, the poet not the play, the figure of Geoffroy rises before me.' As for Dorval, 'I never once took my eyes off her . . . I leaned motionless against the front of the box, a prey to feelings I never experienced before and I felt as if I should choke. . . .'

Emotion reached its highest pitch at the moment of the *dégringolade*. There was a gasp of terror as, distraught and pale, Kitty Bell stumbled to the door of Chatterton's room, only to find that she was too late, that he had taken poison; then with an anguished cry she fell backwards over the banister, and toppled head first, arms outstretched, from top to bottom of the staircase, to crumble dying at its foot.

'Ah,' wrote Théophile Gautier recalling the scene, 'could Chatterton have opened his opium laden eyes one last time on such an abandon of grief, he would have died happy, sure of being loved as no man ever was and that he would not long await his sister soul below.'

The message of *Chatterton* had been received with acclamation by those for whom it pleaded – the young intellectuals who thronged the first night, existing perilously in the garrets of Paris, leading *la vie de bohème* for the love of art. The critics, especially those of a conservative nature, were less ready to welcome it. The play was antisocial, it encouraged idleness and self pity.

> Chatterton qui se tue au lieu de travailler!

sneered a parodist,

> Et quelle est la morale enfin? – un escalier!
> Piquante allegorie, admirable symbole
> Qui semble nous montrer comment l'art
>   dégringole . . .*

The strongest attack, a hostile review in the *Revue des Deux Mondes* condemning the play on moral and intellectual grounds, met with angry reactions from the Romantics. One enthusiast had to be restrained from challenging the critic to a duel; Alfred de Musset and George Sand wrote indignant sonnets, Musset comparing the critic to an inflated bullfrog, George Sand proclaiming the primacy of emotion,

> Quand vous aurez prouvé, messieurs du journalisme,
> Que Chatterton eut tort de mourir ignoré . . .
> Vous n'aurez pas prouvé que je n'ai pas pleuré . . .†

Vigny proudly copied both sonnets into his journal.

---

* Chatterton, who kills himself in place of working! And what is the moral then? – a staircase! Piquant allegory, admirable symbol, which seems to show us how art is tumbling down. . . .

† Gentlemen of the press, when you have proved that Chatterton was wrong to die unknown . . . you will not have proved that I did not weep. . . .

Two months after the first night the play appeared in print. With it, as a tribute to the poet whose name he had used, Vigny included an appreciation of Chatterton's poetry and a selection from his work:

I have seen in an ancient church in Normandy [he wrote] a mound of stones, placed there in expiation by order of Pope Leo X above the body of a young man put to death in error. Less lasting than those stones may this play stand nonetheless as a BOOK OF EXPIATION, to the memory of the young poet. May we in France, above all, show a compassion that is not sterile for those whose destiny resembles that of Chatterton, who died at eighteen years old ...

Vigny's own compassion was never in doubt. The mission imposed on him by Chatterton – the succour and encouragement of young poets – remained a life-long preoccupation. Visitors to his *salon* complained that since *Chatterton* it had become so invaded by *poètes maudits* that it was little more than a 'mental clinic, or employment agency for intellectuals'. But his protégés repaid him with devotion. Flaubert, in the materialistic years of the Second Empire, spoke of him as the sole consoling and comforting figure in the world of letters; and it is moving to think of him, already old and stricken with his last illness, befriending Baudelaire, whose genius he recognized and applauded.

Naturally withdrawn and shunning public life, Vigny's concern for the encouragement of poets and poetry drew him reluctantly into the public arena. In the Academy he fought and intrigued for those he considered deserving. In the press he pleaded vehemently for laws against the exploitation of authors. An open letter to '*Messieurs les Deputés*' in the *Revue des Deux Mondes* of 1841 led to the introduction of a bill to improve the copyright position of authors, and to provide a government pension for three years for any poet who had produced a work of accepted merit. Despite an eloquently argued debate the bill was rejected by an unsympathetic majority, 'a chamber of clerks and grocers' noted Vigny. Balzac, who with Vigny had been listening to the debate from the spectators' benches – the only other writer present – called across with genial resignation:

'Eh bien! monsieur de Vigny, les poètes seront donc toujours, comme l'a dit votre Chatterton, des *parias intelligents?*'*

In 1857, twenty-two years after the famous first night, Théophile Gautier, now an established man of letters, attended a revival of *Chatterton*. Marie Dorval was long since dead, but Geoffroy again took the title role, aged by twenty years (which, said Gautier, is perhaps too much for a poet of eighteen) but still preserving that bitter, fatal and romantic aspect which had captivated the audience of 1835.

But what a change of audience – no longer the wild-eyed young men, no longer the pallid young women with their drooping ringlets who, at the sight of coarse red-faced John Bell, had turned their eyes with melancholy recognition towards the well fed husbands at their sides. The girls in the audience now, said Gautier, would never look at Chatterton – a young man without a penny, skinny, shabbily clad, always declaiming poetry. As for those lords and lord mayors who called on Chatterton, he should think himself lucky, a maniac like that, that they paid the slightest attention to him. Young lords had better things to do these days than to climb up garret stairs.

Vigny's plea for the poet, said Gautier, was basically impractical. He had called upon society to give the poet the time and the bread which he needs to follow his muse. But who is to judge which poet to support, how long must he be kept in idleness until inspiration descends from the sky? Should we take the poet's own word for his genius, or that of popular opinion? If we take the second, the poet, presumably, is no longer in need of support.

Life was sobering the Romantics. 'Ah, how many times must Vigny have blamed himself for preaching that absurd cause . . . Society owes nobody, and above all a child of eighteen, more than the price of their services, not that which they put on their dreams,' wrote Lamartine.

The message of Chatterton was no longer fashionable. But the play had been famous all over Europe, translated into German

---

* 'Ah well! monsieur de Vigny, does that mean that poets will still be, as your Chatterton puts it, *intelligent pariahs?*'

and Italian, played in French at St Petersburg. Its fame lingered and as late as 1876 caught the imagination of the young composer Ruggiero Leoncavallo, then eighteen, a budding poet as well as musician, who turned to Chatterton as the hero of his first opera.

Based on Vigny's play, the story of the opera strayed still further from the real facts of Chatterton's life. Leoncavallo, in this, as in all his operas, was his own librettist; his version of *Chatterton* is very much his own, revealing already the theatrical flair that would reach its brilliant climax in *Pagliacci*.

He achieves his best effects by contrast: the sound of Christmas carols drifts in through the window of Chatterton's garret, where the boy poet, starving, searching vainly for inspiration to write the poems that will pay his debts, finds that the fact of hunger obliterates thoughts of poetry; a group of jesting milords laughs and sings outside as Chatterton, already poisoned, gasps out his dying love for Jenny, his landlord's wife. Only the final effect, the famous *dégringolade*, could not be improved upon. Leoncavallo's heroine, like Vigny's, opens the door of Chatterton's room, to find she is too late, that he is dead; then stumbling backwards, falls head first down the staircase, to lie insensible at its foot, a lifeless figure as the curtain falls.

In Bologna, where Leoncavallo, having just graduated from the Naples Conservatoire, had gone to attend the lectures of the famous poet Carducci, he completed his opera and arranged for its presentation, unwisely paying in advance. On the eve of the performance the impresario disappeared with the money, leaving the luckless composer penniless, and obliged, to escape the fate of his hero, to turn to any work he could find. Playing in cafés, giving singing and piano lessons, finally becoming a virtuoso pianist in Cairo, Leoncavallo spent years of wandering in Europe and the Middle East, sustained in his vagabond life by his determination to succeed, one day, as a composer of operas. *Pagliacci*, written as a pot-boiler when his fortunes were at their lowest, brought him instant fame in 1892; and in its wake, twenty years after it was first written, *Chatterton* was at last performed, in 1896. It was not well received, and though it was revived several times in Leoncavallo's lifetime, most successfully in France, it has now disappeared into operatic limbo, its chief interest that of having provided a disastrous start to its composer's career.

But Vigny's *Chatterton* is accepted as a classic, still performed from time to time, still evoking the romantic memory of his love for Marie Dorval. The *poète maudit,* as personified by Chatterton, is a faintly ridiculous figure, but the clash between the egotism of the bourgeois and the distress of the intellectual still has its appeal for French audiences, above all – as Vigny's editor Baldensperger remarks – when a discreet sentimental intrigue is added to the picture of the poet's plight.

13 The Pre-Raphaelite Image

With Shakespeare's manhood at a boy's wild heart, –
Through Hamlet's doubt to Shakespeare near allied,
And kin to Milton in his Satan's pride, –
At Death's sole door he stooped and craved a dart,
And to that dear new bower of England's art –
Even to that shrine Time else had deified,
The unuttered shrine that strove against his aside,
Drove the fell point, and smote life's seals apart.
Thy nested home-loves, noble Chatterton,
The angel-trodden stair thy soul could trace
Up Redcliffe's spire; and in the world's armed space
Thy gallant sword play: – these to many an one
Are sweet forever; as thy grave unknown
And love-dream of thine unrecorded face.

DANTE GABRIEL ROSSETTI (1881)

The Pre-Raphaelite's idea of the Middle Ages had a connection, though a distant one, with Chatterton, for its spirit derived as much from the English Romantic poets as from the fourteenth-century painters to whose principles, in theory, they wished to return – and Chatterton, according to Dante Gabriel Rossetti, had been 'the day spring' of English Romantic poetry. Rowley's band of craftsmen, poets and painters, united in a common love of art, are shadowy ancestors of the boisterous Pre-Raphaelite brethren.

Chatterton himself, though no longer a Romantic common-place as he had been earlier in the century, could still be seen as a symbol of the creative artist's isolation in a philistine and material-istic world; to the Pre-Raphaelites, in a society increasingly dominated by the Industrial Revolution, the symbolism seemed stark enough.

It was this symbolic aspect that Henry Wallis crystallized in his lovely painting 'Chatterton', one of the minor masterpieces of the Pre-Raphaelite Movement, and still the image which his name most readily evokes. 'The cruelty of the world towards poor Chatterton,' wrote Holman Hunt in his history of Pre-Raphaelitism, '... will never henceforward be remembered without recognition of Henry Wallis, the painter, who first so pathetically excited pity for his state'.

The story of Chatterton was already in the air when Wallis's painting was first exhibited, at the Royal Academy, in 1856. *Chatterton: The Story of a Year*, a biographical novelette by David Masson, had been published earlier that year, a reprint from the *Dublin University Magazine* of 1851. Racy and readable, it set Chatterton against the background of 1770, conjuring up the turbulent politics of the day, the coffee-houses and the taverns, the rival newspapers, the literary scene. It evoked those gloomy last months, when, apart from his letters, so little is known of his life; and that final evening when Chatterton, returning from a solitary ramble through the town, climbed the narrow stairs to his attic room:

He entered and locked the door behind him. – The Devil was abroad that night in the sleeping city. Down narrow and squalid courts his presence was felt, where savage men seized miserable women by the throat, and the neighbourhood was roused by yells of murder, the barking of dogs and the shrieks of children. Up in wretched garrets his presence was felt, where solitary mothers gazed on their infants and longed to kill them. He was in the niches of dark bridges, where outcasts lay huddled together, and some of them stood up from time to time and looked over at the dim stream below. He was in the uneasy hearts of undiscovered forgers and of ruined men plotting mischief. He was in prison-cells, where condemned men condoled with each other in obscene songs and blasphemy. What he achieved that night, in and about that vast city, came duly out into light and history. But of all the spots over which the Black Shadow hung, the chief, for that night at least, was a certain undistinguished house in the narrow street which thousands who now dwell in London pass and repass, scarce observing it, every day of their lives, as they come and go along the thoroughfare of Holborn. At the door of one house in that street the horrid Shape watched; through that door he passed in towards midnight; and from that door, having done his work, he emerged before it was morning.

It was fine dramatic writing, and the book, either on its earlier appearance or in that same year, almost certainly had its effect on Wallis. Typically Pre-Raphaelite in its attention to historical accuracy, details such as the *Middlesex Journal* thrown aside on the floor in the painting may well have derived from it. Typically Pre-Raphaelite too are the strident colours of the picture, the dark red hair, the almost religious atmosphere. The boy poet lies outstretched on his bed, pale and beautiful, like a figure from a *pietà*. A phial of poison has fallen from his hand, scraps of torn-up manuscript are scattered on the floor, through the dusty window, misty in the distance, can be seen the dome of Saint Paul's. Two lines from Marlowe's *Doctor Faustus* are printed beneath the picture:

> Cut is the branch which might have grown full
>   straight
> And burned Apollo's laurel bough . . .

'There is not a trait in the most inanimate part of the picture that does not bear upon the story and enforce its moral,' wrote a Bristol newspaper. 'Faultless and wonderful,' wrote Ruskin, 'a most noble example of the great school. Examine it well, inch by inch; it is one of the pictures which intend and accomplish the entire placing before your eyes of an actual fact and that a solemn one.'

Henry Wallis, at the time of 'Chatterton', was a genial and attractive young artist, who had been caught up in the Pre-Raphaelite orbit – and whose most successful work was done under the influence of their style. He was popular in literary as well as artistic circles. The young George Meredith and his wife were close friends and Meredith, then twenty-seven and just beginning to be known as a writer, posed as his model for the painting; the Gray's Inn chambers of another friend were used for the garret setting.

Meredith's friendship with Wallis, captured in the Chatterton painting, was not to last. Two years later his wife eloped with

Wallis to Capri, a double betrayal by wife and friend. The situation had its parallel in another Pre-Raphaelite triangle when Millais, while painting Ruskin, fell in love with his wife, whom he later married. For Mrs Meredith there was no such happy ending. Deserted soon after by Wallis, she died unreconciled with Meredith.

The break-up of the marriage, with its progression of disillusion, was the theme of Meredith's sonnet sequence 'Modern Love':

> Ah, what a dusty answer gets the soul
> When hot for certainties in this our life.

In the last years of his life Dante Gabriel Rossetti thought much about the Romantic poets, in whose treatment by a hostile world he saw a reflection of his own. 'Men of intelligence in England are ever as a persecuted sect,' he commented sadly. The ebullience of his youth had largely left him. Drugged by chloral, which he took in increasing doses to combat insomnia and ill-health, and which in turn compounded both, his sense of persecution had become abnormal. Attacks on his work in the press castigating the 'fleshliness' of his art had driven him to attempt suicide. He felt himself surrounded by enemies, a pariah. Once an enthusiastic Cockney, never happier than when roaming its streets, he now saw London as base and impersonal, destructive in its indifference:

> A city of sweet speech scorned, on whose chill stone
> Keats withered; Coleridge pined; and Chatterton,
> Breadless with poison froze the god-fired breath ...

His devotion to Chatterton – 'excessive and fanciful,' thought his brother – owed something to the context of his own unhappiness. But it was above all that of a poet. 'Nothing', said Hall Caine in his *Recollections of Dante Gabriel Rossetti*, 'would suffice him but that I should go down on my knees and worship the author of the "African Eclogues".' 'Are you up in his work?' asked Rossetti early in their correspondence, 'he is in the very first rank.' When Caine rashly suggested that Oliver Brown, the gifted son of Ford Madox Brown, who had recently died, had enough genius to stock a good few Chattertons, he was sharply taken to task:

You must take care to be on the right track about Chatterton. . . . Those who compare nett results in cases such as his and Chatterton's cannot know what criticism means. . . . Oliver was the product of the most teeming hotbeds of art and literature. . . . What he would have become if, like the ardent and heroic Chatterton, he had had to fight a single handed battle for art and bread together against a merciless mediocrity in high places – what he would then have become I cannot in the least calculate; but we know what Chatterton became.

Caine suggested that Chatterton was lacking in the note of 'personal purity and majesty of character', in short of sincerity. 'I must protest finally about Chatterton,' replied Rossetti,

The finest of the Rowley poems – Eclogues, Ballad of Charity etc. – rank absolutely with the finest poetry in the language. As to what you say about C.'s want of political sincerity (for I cannot see to what other want you allude) surely a boy of eighteen may be pardoned for exercising his faculty if he happens to be the one among millions who can use grown men as his toys. He was an absolute and untarnished hero. . . .

Like Keats, Rossetti drew a parallel between Chatterton and Shakespeare. He was, he declared, 'the only man in England's theatre of imagination who could have bandied parts with Shakespeare'. He repeated the comparison in his lovely sonnet,

> With Shakespeare's manhood at a boy's wild heart –
> Through Hamlet's doubt to Shakespeare near
> allied . . .

He offered this sonnet, one of five on the Romantic poets written about this time, to his friend Theodore Watts, to use as a preface to the appreciation of Chatterton he had been commissioned to write for *Ward's English Poets*, published in 1880. But Watts, though deeply indebted to Rossetti for the material in his essay, did not feel he could go the whole way with this comparison and did not use the sonnet.

Theodore Watts (later Watts-Dunton), the literary lawyer, was, in Rossetti's words, a 'hero of friendship', memorable for his devotion to disorderly genius. Already at 'The Pines', Putney, Swinburne was installed under his kindly wing. The Bacchic excesses of the fiery red-haired poet had gone too far. Rossetti had his own memories of Swinburne as a housemate – sliding down the banisters naked, flinging a poached egg at Meredith, a fellow-lodger, because he spoke disrespectfully of Victor Hugo. Now with Watts, sensitive, tactful and proprietary, to supervise, the weaning to a daily bottle of Bass had begun.

For Rossetti, Watts's friendship was equally solicitous. He dined with him several times a week, distracted him from melancholy, and since he was now handling his affairs, was invaluable in coping with the many problems of his disorganized life. Rossetti, who respected his critical judgement as well as his business acumen, would discuss his poetry and painting with him, and in return was generous in furthering Watts's own literary career. When Watts was commissioned to write on Chatterton, Rossetti was quick to offer assistance. 'I am glad you are doing Chatterton,' he wrote, 'he was a glorious creature.' When Watts at dinner one evening suggested that Chatterton was *difficile,* Rossetti defended him warmly. 'Well, I suppose he was proud – poets *are* proud – "And kin to Milton in his Satan's pride".'

He set himself to 'get up' the subject for his friend, borrowing or buying all the available works on the poet. Using the Southey Cottle collected edition of his poetry, and the recent modernizations of the 'Antiques' by the eminent philologist Professor Skeat, he worked on his own adaptations of the poems for the selection included with Watts's article, since Skeat, though a sound scholar, was 'no hand at all' when it came to substituting archaisms in the text. He listed the poems in order of merit, beginning with 'The Ballad of Charity', the 'Eclogues' and the songs from *Aella.* He praised the Byronic wit and impudence of the political pieces, and the rollicking mixture of wit, ingenuity and every kind of fun in *The Revenge.* He saw the importance of Chatterton as a germinating influence in later poets, pointing out the analogies between the 'Ballad of Charity' and Keats's 'Eve of Saint Agnes'; the similarity of certain images with those of Blake; the relationship between the 'Antiques' and Coleridge's 'Christabel', and the mysterious suggestiveness of the place-names in the 'African Eclogues', evoking the 'world involving echoes of "Kubla Khan".'

These parallels and much other material supplied by Rossetti were used by Watts in his completed essay, the finest nineteenth-century assessment of Chatterton's place in English literature; drawing attention to Chatterton's metrical originality, which as much as the Romantic temper of his work had influenced his successors, Watts claimed for Chatterton the place of 'father of the New English Romantic School'.

The keynote of Chatterton's work, he said, was his power of artistic self-effacement, the wonderful impersonality, so unlacharacteristic of the very young, with which he viewed his subject. It was this self-effacement that lay behind his forgeries: Chatterton was a born artist, 'so dominated by the artist's yearning to represent that if perfect representation seemed to demand forgery he needs must forge'.

In his final paragraph, after a short account of Chatterton's life, he turned once more to the vexed question of Chatterton's motives:

It is not to make capital out of the painful interest attaching to Chatterton's life that I glance at it here on his behalf. . . . To divest 'the marvellous boy' of that sensational kind of interest which has been associated with his name for more than a century, and at the same time do justice to an intelligence which Malone compared with Shakespeare's, and a genius which inspired Wordsworth and Coleridge with awe, would require an exhaustive study of that most puzzling chapter of literary history – the chapter that deals with literary forgery. And my defence of him is simply this: that, if such a study were prosecuted, we should find that in matters of literary forgery, besides the impulse of the mere mercenary impostor – as Chatterton appears to empirical critics like Warton – besides the impulse of the masquerading instinct, so strong in men of the Ireland and Horace Walpole type, there is another impulse altogether, the impulse of certain artistic natures to represent, such as we see in Sir Walter Scott (when tampering with the historical ballads), and such as we see in Chatterton when, struggling in his dark garret with famine and despair, he turns from the hackwork that might at least win him bread, to write 'The Ballad of Charity', the most purely artistic work perhaps of his time.

14 The Opportune Ghost

Come listen to my roundelaie,
Come droppe the brinie tear with me.
For Stephannon has gone awaye,
And long away perchance will be!
Our friend he is sicke,
Gone to take physicke,
Al in the infirmarie. . . .

We ne'er shall see his lyke agenne,
We ne'er agenne his lyke shall see,
Searche among al Englishe menne,
You ne'er will find the lyke of hee.
Our friende he is sicke,
Gone to take physicke,
Al in the infirmarie.

FRANCIS THOMPSON, following Chatterton's 'Minstrels' Roundelay'

The nineteenth century drew to a close. Victorian Romanticism
passed into its final stage. The poet Francis Thompson, though
set aside by his Catholicism and the asceticism of his life, did not
escape the spirit of his age. The exalted imagery of 'The Hound of
Heaven' and the raptures of his religious poetry are typically *fin
de siècle*. Nonetheless he delved deep into the work of earlier
poets, and Chatterton, both as a poet and a fellow-sufferer in the
heartless streets of London, was to have a special significance in
his life.

In his lighter moments Francis Thompson could display an
endearing turn for humorous verse. Chatterton must first have
caught his fancy as a schoolboy, for one of his earliest attempts in
this medium was the parody of the 'Willow Song', quoted above,
written on the occasion of a master's illness. The master's name
was Stephannon, the school Ushaw, a Catholic public school to

which his parents, devout converts both, had sent him at the age of twelve. ('The Church of Rome,' Chatterton had written in his creed, 'is certainly the true Church.' Here was another point for sympathy.)

The habit of parody, unfortunately for Thompson's reputation, was close to the habit of plagiarism. Steeped in English poetry from his earliest years, and with a retentive memory, he was all too inclined, consciously or subsconsciously, to echo the words and ideas of others. 'If Crashaw, Shelley, Donne, Marvell, Patmore and some others had not existed, Francis Thompson would be a poet of remarkable novelty,' wrote A. J. A. Symons, when his first book of poems appeared.

Literary allusions not only pervaded his work, they pervaded his life as well. De Quincey provides a typical instance. It was his mother's gift of De Quincey's *Confessions of an English Opium Eater*, that first sped Thompson on the road to laudanum addiction as a medical student in Manchester, and from then on the parallels between the two writers became too many to be incidental. De Quincey, like Thompson, came from Manchester. After six years of wasted studies, missed lectures and drug-induced indolence, Thompson, already a failed candidate for the priesthood, failed his medical exams as well; he fled from Manchester and his understandably exasperated father to London, and, like De Quincey – and Chatterton – plunged into its lowest depths.

His mother had died, but his father, Doctor Thompson, was kind, if unimaginative. There was no question of rejection; he had given no indication of literary ambitions. But he left, without a word of explanation, impelled by a kind of death-wish, for the life of the gutter. He was twenty-six. For two years he led a life of utter penury. Like De Quincey he found excuses, real or imagined, for avoiding any employment suitable to his talents. His father sent him a weekly order for seven shillings, but after a while he ceased to collect it, fearing, he said, that one day it would not be there. He sought only to exist, wandering aimlessly through the streets, making the pittance he needed to live – and to buy the laudanum that was as necessary as food – by calling cabs, blacking boots, selling matches. He slept when he had the money in doss-houses, if not in the open, constantly moved on by the police. He became an adept at husbanding his pennies. 'No Evvie,' he said to his biographer Everard Meynell years later:

You do not spend your penny on a mug of tea. That will be gone very quickly. You spend it Evvie, not on a mug of tea; not, I say on a *mug* of tea, but on the tea itself. You buy a pennyworth and make it with the boiling water from the common kettle in the doss house. You get several cups that way instead of one.

For a time he was able to read in the Guildhall public library, till his scarecrow appearance caused him to be turned away. Dazed and decrepit from laudanum, lack of food and broken nights, he found himself caught in his self-sought misery, tasting 'the life that is not a life; to which food is as the fuel of hunger; sleep, our common sleep, precious, costly and fallible as water in a wilderness; in which men rob and women vend themselves – for fourpence'.

At his lowest ebb, he was befriended and sheltered by a woman of the streets – De Quincey, too, was tended by a prostitute. De Quincey's Anne had disappeared one day into the London streets, sought but never to be found again. So, too, Thompson's benefactress was to disappear, sacrificing herself when fame knocked at his door. 'They will not understand our friendship, I always knew you were a genius,' she said. But that was still to come.

Through all, Thompson was sustained by the drug, his dreams and poetry. His was the vision that could see

the traffic of Jacob's ladder
Pitched betwixt heaven and Charing Cross

and in the corner of doss-houses he would write his poetry. Then, a windfall of a few shillings providing him with a breathing-space, he composed a long and erudite essay on the subject of 'Paganism, Old and New', rich with learned allusions and quotations from the classics, and written 'in the unharassed manner of a man whose style, and cuffs, had been kept in order at the Savile Club'. Coming to his last page and his last halfpenny together, he dropped poems and manuscript, with a burst of

K

uncharacteristic decision, into the letter box of *Merrie England*, a Catholic magazine dealing with the arts and current affairs, edited by Wilfrid Meynell. His covering letter apologized for the soiled state of the manuscript: 'It is due not to slovenliness, but to the strange places and circumstances under which it has been written. For me no less than Parolles, the dirty nurse experience has something fouled', and it ended with the PS. 'Kindly address your rejection to the Charing Cross Post Office.' Next day he spent the halfpenny on two boxes of matches and began the struggle for life anew.

But the manuscript, so unpromising and dirty, was pigeon-holed without being read. No letter came to the Charing Cross Post Office. Months went by and Thompson, his last hope seemingly failed, reached the breaking-point of endurance. He determined to commit suicide. Then Chatterton intervened. The story, as recounted by Wilfrid Meynell, runs thus:

He used before I knew him to sleep at night under the arches of Covent Garden where every quarter of an hour he was liable to be kicked awake by the police and told to move on. It was in an empty space of ground behind the market that he resolved on suicide. He then spent all his remaining pence on laudanum, one large dose, and he went there one night to take it. He had swallowed half when he felt an arm laid on his wrist and looking up he saw Chatterton standing over him and forbidding him to take the other half. I asked him when he told me of it how had he known it was Chatterton. He said, 'I recognised him from the pictures of him – besides I knew that it was he before I saw him – and I remembered at once the story of the money which arrived for Chatterton the day after his death.

(Thompson here, presumably, was thinking of Doctor Fry.)

Visions of Chatterton's death-bed had filled De Quincey's drug-induced dreams. Francis Thompson took them one step further. The ghostly intervention was startlingly opportune – too opportune to take without a pinch of salt. In Thompson's reminiscences the line between fantasy and real life was shadowy. But the misery and despair were real, just as Chatterton's had been, and the next day brought news which was to be the turning-point in Thompson's life.

A family friend, a priest from Manchester, had tracked Thompson down. He told him that one of the poems, sent with his essay, had been printed in that month's issue of *Merrie England*. Wilfrid Meynell, after long delay, had read his work, and immediately seen the quality of it. But his letters to Thompson were returned unopened – Thompson had long ceased going to the Charing Cross Post Office. In an effort to get in touch with him, Meynell decided to print one of his poems, hoping that Thompson would see it and communicate with him. The stratagem succeeded. Thompson wrote him a letter of dignified reproach, giving the forwarding address of a chemist's shop in Drury Lane. Wilfrid Meynell, convinced that here was a writer of outstanding merit, followed up his letter of explanation – which was unanswered – with a visit to the chemist's shop. Here the chemist presented him with a bill for 3s 9d for laudanum, owed by Thompson, which Meynell paid, and promised, for a further sum, to pass on a message to Thompson should he call again.

Some weeks later Francis Thompson was announced at Meynell's office. Twice he half opened the door and then retreated before he could summon up the courage to enter the room. A figure of appalling destitution greeted Meynell's eyes. Frail and stooping, he was in rags, his bare feet showing through his boots, without a shirt, his coat torn. He seemed in the last stages of physical collapse. To Meynell's question as to how in such a state he had obtained the quotations for his essay, he replied, 'Books I have none, but Blake and the Bible.' All the quotations had been from memory.

Shy and evasive, and clinging obstinately to his liberty, Thompson evaded all Meynell's suggestions of help, consenting only to accept a cheque for the poem and to call again some other time. But the warmth and sensitivity of Wilfrid Meynell, and later of his wife, the poet Alice Meynell, melted Thompson's reserve at later meetings. Gathered into the family circle, packed off to hospital for a cure (never more than partial) for his laudanum addiction, Francis Thompson began to write. Under their gentle and constant influence he published his first book of poems; the rest of his life and writing was carried out under their kindly aegis. Thanks to their promotion he acquired a fame which soared to astonishing heights in the decade before the First World War. (He died, aged forty-three, in 1907.) His poetry is out of favour now; he is chiefly remembered for 'The Hound of Heaven' and the still, grave beauty of 'In No Strange Land', but the Meynells were convinced of his genius. He in his turn, outwardly shy and undemonstrative, never forgot the fateful moment when he stood outside the door of the *Merrie England* office, hoping yet not daring to hope:

> Like one who sweats before a despot's gate,
> Summoned by some presaging scroll of fate,
> And knows not whether kiss or dagger wait. . . .
> At fate's dread portal then,
> Even so stood I, I ken
> Even so stood I, between a joy and fear,
> And said to mine own heart, 'now if the end be
>   here'.

Chatterton had not been so lucky.

15 The Poet Biographer

> ... O grant me this, that ere I stand
> Upon the bright, the farther strand
> Of thy renown I chant one worthy song:
> Then, though no tributary ask
> My name, encouragement or task,
> By fame my Love shall have been made most
> strong.
>
> E. H. W. MEYERSTEIN: 'Song to Chatterton'

The Chatterton myth, with the ideas it had embodied, faded with the end of the Romantic Movement. Francis Thompson, despairing behind the arches of Covent Garden, seemed to have caught its final radiance. Victim of over-exposure, Chatterton passed through cliché into obscurity.

Nonetheless, in the early years of the century he continued to make occasional appearances. The young Vita Sackville-West, aged seventeen, wrote a play in blank verse on Chatterton. Privately printed, it revealed once more his attraction for the young and creative, the 'pale slight boy in dark grey dress' expressing the irritation of youth at the inadequacies of their elders:

> My poor mother came
> And fetched me suddenly away, to talk
> Inanities all through a dragging meal;

and the artist's sense of terror,

> That what he has accomplished is so small
> So infinitely little, when compared
> With what he should have done and still may do.

A German writer, Ernst Penzoldt, wrote a sentimental novel,

Der Arme Chatterton; an American, Esther Parker Ellinger, psycho-
analysed him along Alderian lines as a neurotic. Professor Saintsbury gave serious attention to his poetry in his *History of English
Prosody*. 'A new prosodic inspiration', he wrote, ran through the
Rowley poems; before Blake, Chatterton had restored the lyric
impulse to English poetry. A quatrain such as this:

> I kenne Syr Roger from afar
> Tryppynge o'er the lea;
> Ich ask whie the loverde's son
> Is moe than me

was 'a breath from heaven'.

These were marks of interest, slight enough after the enthusiasms
of the nineteenth century. Then in 1930, after years of near
oblivion, a monumental work appeared, monumental in every
sense, the poet's brief career sustaining a book of nearly six
hundred pages. Modestly entitled *A Life of Thomas Chatterton*, it
is in fact *the* life, the fruit of years of scholarship and research,
unlikely to be surpassed as the standard biography. Myth and
sentimentality are cleared away, Chatterton's character is shown
in an often unpleasing light, but the book, for all its objectivity,
is a work of love. In its author, E. H. W. Meyerstein, Chatterton
had once more found a champion, a poet whose devotion to him,
obsessive in its intensity, linked up with that of the Romantics.
But this was the twentieth century, the Romantic Movement was
dead. Significantly, Chatterton's new champion was a man outside the mainstream of contemporary literature, an odd and
fantastic figure whose standing as a poet, in life as now, was
ambiguous.

Edward Harry William Meyerstein was born in 1889, the
child of ambitious and dominating Jewish parents. At Harrow,
where his background and sensitive, bookish temperament made
him a misfit, he suffered, or felt he suffered, the fate of a pariah.
At Oxford, though a brilliant classical scholar, he failed to get
the First and later the Fellowship he hoped for. Early failures
confirmed in him a life-long sense of injury; a persecution
complex was ever ready to poison his relationships.

Despite this he had a wide and gifted circle of friends. His friendships alone – with figures such as Masefield and de la Mare – implant him in the literary history of the first half of this century. 'No-one who knew Meyerstein could possibly forget him,' writes John Wain, who gives a vivid picture of his later years in *Sprightly Running*. He was a formidable scholar, musician, critic, novelist; an invigorating conversationalist, savage in controversy; a poet with a poet's insight into the workings of the creative mind. But he was a wounded man. His brilliance, his learning, his poetic gifts, were shadowed by torturing melancholia, which clouded and at times threatened to unseat his reason.

As he grew older he became increasingly eccentric, a big shambling figure somewhat in the style of Doctor Johnson, his face distorted with the effects of Bell's Palsy, which had twisted his features to one side. His Gray's Inn chambers, where he lived in disorder and with incredible parsimony, were crowded with priceless old books and manuscripts, his defence against the modernity he loathed. His manners were old-fashioned and courteous, if unconventional – he would wave his false teeth to make a point; his clothes, conventional in intention, were habitually dilapidated. His humour tended towards the macabre. He liked jokes about hangmen (though he abhorred capital punishment); he had a score of anecdotes about murders past and present, would walk for miles to see the scene of a crime. At a different level, themes of murder, pain and violent death ran through his work, signs of the obsessions that burdened his mind and cast a blight on much of his work.

For all his talents, he was never a literary success. His work was too strange, too impregnated with his own obsessions, to be popular, though like that other literary eccentric, Rolfe, with whom he has been compared, he would always appeal to a few. He wrote eleven novels; he contributed to learned journals; he produced an enormous amount of poetry, some of it extremely fine, all the work of an artist steeped in the knowledge of his craft – he was the most distinguished metrist of his day – but none given more than cautious praise by reviewers, or selling more than a few hundred copies. But it was as a poet that he

wished to be remembered; all other literary tasks were subordin-
ated to this ambition. 'His spirits often sank for lack of recognition,'
wrote Professor Lionel Butler in his appreciation of Meyerstein
for the British Academy, 'though he consoled himself that
posterity would find in him the poetic stature to which his
contemporaries had been blind. The example of Chatterton
strongly suggested to him that publicity is not fame, that fame
roots itself most firmly in the grave.'

Was this one of the reasons that drew him so strongly to
Chatterton? There were so many pyschological attractions in his
story. Meyerstein was obsessed by death and suicide, by the idea
of neglected genius, intensely in sympathy with the misfits and
rejects of society. But none of these would have mattered had he
not been convinced of Chatterton's poetic genius.

He first became interested in him in 1915 when, having been
discharged from the army as unsuitable, he was working in the
Manuscripts Room of the British Museum. He had been reading
Chaucer, he wrote to a friend in 1945, and 'it was at this time I
discovered how really good Chatterton's Rowley poems were, in
spite of their faked Old English, because I could read them after
Chaucer'.

Even before he read the poems there had been a moment of
vision. 'I find it hard – perhaps it is a mistake to try – to tell you
what Chatterton has meant to me since about the middle of the
war,' he wrote elsewhere.

I was coming out of a house in Lancaster Gate where people, one of
them a poet, had been talking about poetry – and I said nothing, feeling
they were wrong and knew nothing about poetry or what it really
was, and at last I came away alone. I was just free of the house when
the thought came – 'Chatterton is your *only* hope; he will make you a
poet and no-one else'. I cannot truly say whether it was before or
after that time that I picked up his works in two volumes (Methuen's
edition) in the Queen's Road, Bayswater, for 1s.; but I know this – *that
I had not read them when that thought fired me with hope*. Since then it is
only through him that I can sit among people who write what is
called poetry and feel that I shall live – or rather my work will – when
they are dust and ashes.

In the early 1920s he started work on his life of Chatterton. It was the only biography he ever wrote. Despite his erudition he spurned the reputation which he might have gained as an outstanding literary biographer; poetry absorbed his major energies. But his life of Chatterton was a task he felt enjoined on him by Chatterton's shade. He devoted nine years to bringing it to completion.

In 1928 he installed himself in a room near Saint Mary Redcliffe to pursue his researches in Bristol. He wrote from there: 'As long as I can get near my idea – my vision of Thomas Chatterton, irrespective of what I may produce about him, I know interior happiness . . .' And in a note written as he waited in the church for the verger: 'I don't think I shall be able to tell you much about this work I am on now. It has a sort of silencing power.' The beauty of the church seized his imagination. 'It is very easy to romanticize about Chatterton, fatally easy, and I am as great a sinner in that respect as any – but consider the effect of living under a great church like Saint Mary Redcliffe, and knowing your ancestors had been sextons of it "time out of mind" would be on any sensitive child.'

> He who would look upon thy smile
> Must traverse Redcliffe's Canynged aisle
> And raise from it the Gothic o his grief

he wrote in his 'Song to Chatterton'.

His chief problem, he found, in writing his book (politics and accuracy apart) was to be fair to Chatterton's mother and sister 'out of an innate suspicion that all *women,* relations included are the unwitting worst enemies of the creative type'. Throughout his life Meyerstein had a deep-rooted and often expressed distrust of the opposite sex. He falls over backward to be fair in his book, but there is a false sweetness in his picture of Chatterton's family life. Far more in character is the acidulous tone of a footnote such as this, on Fanny Burney's opinion of Michael Lort, the scholar, as 'a man altogether out of the common road without having discovered a better path': 'A typically feminine judgement of a man only concerned with the truth'; or this, dismissing Vigny's

Chatterton: 'I am unable to say whether it holds the stage but I believe it is played in girls' schools.'

The book was respectfully received when it appeared and though it never achieved a wide readership its reputation has been lasting. 'Legends fall before his advance,' wrote *The Times Literary Supplement*. 'The Chatterton who is made visible in Mr Meyerstein's book is probably as near the original as any study we shall ever receive.' From a mass of voluminous and painstaking scholarship the greatest importance of the book was the death-blow it dealt, once and for all, to the sentimental picture of Chatterton as a hapless child victim. Meyerstein's view of Chatterton's character, after years of research, accorded closely to the summing up of an eighteenth-century biographical dictionary: 'This unfortunate person, though certainly a most extraordinary genius seems yet to have been of a most ungracious composition. He was violent and impetuous to a strange degree . . . he appears to have had a portion of ill humour and spleen more than enough for a youth of seventeen.'

Walpole's dealings with Chatterton were sympathetically presented. Meyerstein's character had obvious affinities with Walpole's, and his love for Chatterton did not prevent him from putting Walpole's point of view in detail or suggesting that Chatterton's role, in this instance, was less that of a victim than that of 'a bold presumptuous decoy duck on his mettle'.

Barrett and Catcott, Chatterton's dupes, were, he opined, not altogether deceived; admittedly convinced that Chatterton's discoveries were genuine, they probably suspected him of 'cooking up' or improving on them.

On the subject of Chatterton's antique language he was emphatic:

We do the author of *Aella* no service by modernising his antiques to the slightest extent. If for instance we write *honour* for his *honnoure* we are losing the weight of the first syllable and the resonance of the second.

> Hong pendaunte bie thy sworde and crave for thy
> morth

is ruined as word music when replaced by

      Hung pendant by thy sword & c.

No! leave the 'olde rouste' alone and read him aloud, not with the eye merely, and out of that barbarous incantation emerge the indisputable form and stature of an English poet.

The book was dedicated, as 'Endymion' had been, to the memory of Chatterton; and at the end, as he spoke of Chatterton's tragedy, he expressed his own feelings on the writing of poetry which is, in most cases, its own reward: 'The one laurel, which unencouraged genius, or talent, can wrest from his contemporaries, is doggedly and humbly to have persisted in life, seeing that fame, the sure end of merit, is of its very nature, a quiet and an immaterial thing.'

He did not set himself beside Chatterton, but he felt his case, as a poet out of step with his time, to be similar. 'There have been at all times certain writers and poets who run counter to the influence of their time, and have been forced out of it, either to death, like Chatterton, insanity like Smart, or the suspicion of insanity i.e. eccentricity like Blake,' he wrote in 1944. '. . . I have very little doubt that I am a writer of that class and I begin to be frightened of what will happen to me. . . .' As he grew older the moods of despair and disappointment grew blacker and more frequent. He thought of death continually, yet he would not entertain, as Chatterton had done, the idea of suicide. 'There is one ethical command,' he wrote in his journal, '– YOU MUST NOT KILL YOURSELF. However unbearable your environment is you must not do that.'

But the temptation was there. Alone and sleepless in his Holborn room one night, his brain obsessed by doubts and fears, the vision of Chatterton appeared to him as it had appeared to Francis Thompson, a pitying figure, his face marked with sorrow, bidding him take courage, for all the hopelessness that overwhelmed him:

> Not many yards from this your lonely bed
> A lonelier than you broke life's locked door,
> And when the shades of fatal night were fled

They found his papers piecemeal on the floor,
The limbs and face distorted of the dead,
Who had no sense of what his days were for,
But now remembers and bids you live on,
Your guardian angel Thomas Chatterton.*

For Meyerstein the vision was real, the idea of Chatterton was one that sustained him throughout his life. He carried in his pocket, like a talisman, a scrap of Chatterton's writing. He took him as his poetic touchstone: 'No poet assures me of my integrity quite as Chatterton does.' He referred to him continually in his poetry. Even in his novels he could not resist the idea of Chatterton: allusions to him and his work are recurring features. And when the long struggle for fame seemed most hopeless, he could still see in Chatterton the prospect of immortality:

... All that is good
In me is due to him
He rides manhood
As God the Cherubim.
Beneath his tightening rein
I shall arrive
Where others with more pain
Can hardly strive.

Full many an one
Shall raise the song o'er me
In abbey none
Although I buried be;
And if I have a stone
Be carved on it:
'One Thomas Chatterton
Tuned this man's wit'.†

Meyerstein died in 1952. In his will he endowed a 'Chatterton Lecture', to be given yearly at the British Academy, on an English poet no longer living. Fittingly, he was himself the subject of the first lecture.

---

* 'Chatterton in Holborn: A Vision'.
† 'Pride'.

His collection of books and manuscripts was bequeathed to libraries; the Chattertoniana, with his own heavily annotated copy of the biography – he was revising and adding to it up to the year of his death – went to the Bristol Central Library. Another annotated copy is in the British Museum, and in the Manuscripts Room there are notes on Chatterton in his small neat hand. If Chatterton has not yet won him fame as a poet, he has already ensured his niche as a scholar.

The story of Chatterton ends on a dying fall. The poet whom Keats and Coleridge loved, whose legend caught the Romantic imagination, found in the lonely and unfulfilled figure of Meyerstein his sole significant champion in the twentieth century. But his myth, though forgotten, is not irrelevant. Chatterton, starving in his garret, is the precursor of the cult figures of our own time – actors, musicians, revolutionaries, whose early death has made them symbols. Youth and death are a powerful combination. In Chatterton's case they were linked to poetic genius. The poetry remains, more lasting than the legend.

Books Consulted

Chatterton, Thomas, *Poems supposed to have been written by T.Rowley and others*, ed. Tyrwhitt (1777); *Miscellanies* (1778); *Collected Works*, ed. Southey and Cottle (1803); *The Poetical Works*, ed. Skeat (1871); *Complete Poetical Works*, ed. H. D. Roberts (1906); *The Complete Works of Thomas Chatterton*, ed. D. S. Taylor (1971).

Barrett, William, *History of Bristol*, Bristol (1789).
Bird, C. W., *Alfred de Vigny's Chatterton: its genesis and sources*, Los Angeles (1941).
Browning, Robert, *Essay on Chatterton*, ed. S.Donald Smalley, Cambridge, Mass. (1948).
Bryant, Jacob, *Observations upon the poems of Rowley* (1781).
Butler, Lionel, 'The Chatterton Lecture', British Academy (1955).
Caine, T. Hall, *Recollections of Dante Gabriel Rossetti* (1882).
Cambridge History of English Literature (1913), x, ch.10.
Chambers, E. K., *S. T.Coleridge* (1950).
Clarke, Ernest, *New Lights on Chatterton* (1913).
Coleridge, S. T., *Complete Poetical Works*, ed. E. H. Coleridge (1912).
Cottle, Joseph, *Malvern Hills* (1829); *Early Recollections* (1837); *Reminiscences of Coleridge and Southey* (1847).
Cremer, R. W. Ketton, *Horace Walpole* (1940).
Croft, Herbert, *Love and Madness* (1780).
Dix, John, *The Life of Thomas Chatterton* (1837).
Dixon, W. Macneile, 'Warton Lecture on English Poetry', British Academy (1930).
Doughty, Oswald, *Dante Gabriel Rossetti, A Victorian Romantic* (1949).
Ellinger, Esther Parker, *Thomas Chatterton*, Philadelphia (1930).
Gaunt, William, *The Pre-Raphaelite Tragedy* (1942).
Gautier, Théophile, *Histoire du Romantisme*, Paris (1874).
Gittings, Robert, *John Keats* (1968).
Gosse, Edmund, *History of Eighteenth Century English Literature* (1889).
Grebanier, Bernard, *The Great Shakespeare Forgery* (1966).
Gregory, G., 'Life of Chatterton', *Biographia Britannica* (1789).
Grove's Musical Dictionary, 'Leoncavallo' (1964).

Haller, William, *The Early Life of Robert Southey* (1917).

Houghton, Lord, *The Life and Letters of John Keats* (1848).

Hunt, W. Holman, *Pre-Raphaelitism and the Pre-Raphaelite Brotherhood* (1905).

Ingram, J. H., *The True Chatterton* (1910).

Ireland, W. H., *Confessions* (1805); *Neglected Genius* (1812).

Jenkins, Elizabeth, *Ten Fascinating Women*, chapter relating to Martha Ray (1955).

Keats, John, *Poems*, ed. E. de Selincourt (1905); *Letters*, ed. M. Buxton Forman (1947).

Knight, J., *Life of Rossetti* (1881).

Lauvrière, Emile, *Alfred de Vigny, sa vie et son œuvre*, Paris (1945).

Mair, J. *The Fourth Forger* (1938).

Maitland, R. S., *Chatterton: An Essay* (1857) (pamphlet).

Malone, Edmond, *Observations on the Poems of Thomas Rowley* (1782).

Masson, David, *A Story of the Year 1770* (1856).

Meyerstein, E. H. W., *A Life of Thomas Chatterton* (1930); *Of my early life, 1889–1918*, ed. R. Watson (1957); *Some Letters*, ed. R. Watson (1959); *Some Poems*, ed. M. Wollman (1960).

Meynell, Everard, *Life of Francis Thompson* (1913).

Milles, Jeremiah, *Poems . . . by Thomas Rowley* (1782).

Praz, Mario, *The Romantic Agony* (1933).

Quennell, Peter, *Romantic England* (1970).

Rodway, Alan, *The Romantic Conflict* (1963).

Rollins, H. E. (ed.), *The Keats Circle* (1948).

Rossetti, Dante Gabriel, *Correspondence*, ed. O. Doughty and J. Wahl (1967) IV; *Collected Works*, ed. W. M. Rossetti (1886).

Saintsbury, George, *History of English Prosody* (1910), II and III.

de la Salle, Bertrand, *Alfred de Vigny*, Paris (1963).

Sassoon, Siegfried, *Life of Meredith* (1948).

Simmons, J., *Southey* (1945).

Streatfield, R., *Masters of Italian Music* (1895).

de Vigny, Alfred, *Oeuvres Completes*, ed. F. Baldensperger, Paris (1964).

Wain, John, *Sprightly Running* (1962) (chapter relating to Meyerstein).

Walpole, Horace, *Correspondence* ed. W. S. Lewis (1952) XVI; *Letters*, selected W. S. Lewis (1951).

Walsh, John, *Strange Harp, Strange Symphony* (1968) (Life of Francis Thompson).

Ward, Aileen, *John Keats: The Making of a Poet* (1963).

Ward's English Poets, Chatterton (1880), III.

Whitridge, Arnold, *Alfred de Vigny* (1933).
Wilson, Daniel, *Chatterton: A Biographical Study* (1869).
Winwar, F., *Farewell the Banner* (1939) (early years of Coleridge and Wordsworth).

OTHER SOURCES

Chatterton Mss. in the British Museum.
Cuttings and letters relating to Chatterton in the British Museum and Bristol Central Library.
George Catcott's Letter Book in the Bristol Central Library.
W. H. Ireland Mss. in the British Museum.
Vocal score of Leoncavallo's *Chatterton* (1906) (French version).
Wanlass, Dorothy Clare, *Chatterton: Controversy and Legend*, doctoral thesis, Columbia University (1961).

I have also referred to various magazines and periodicals all of which are mentioned in the text.

Index